THE REFINED HOME

SHELDON HARTE

THE REFINED HOME
SHELDON HARTE

TEXT BY MITCHELL OWENS AND HADLEY KELLER

VENDOME

NEW YORK · LONDON

CONTENTS

As a child, I told my father that I wanted to be either a haberdasher or own a Cadillac dealership when I grew up. But my career as an interior designer seems to have been preordained. Growing up in Southern California with a father who designed landscapes and pools and a mother in the fashion industry who used to take me antiquing with her, I was surrounded by a resourceful ingenuity.

My parents had good taste, and they appreciated an attractive home life. The house they built in the San Fernando Valley, shortly before I was born, was a Cliff May plan that the influential ranch-house architect sold through magazines. It was simple, modern, and made of wood, and even when I was young, I was aware that it looked nothing like any of our friends' houses. The exterior was painted what my mother called "old-money green," a mossy color with a bit of brown in it, the carpet in the living room was Sauternes green, my bedroom was decorated with a toile de Jouy, and the floors were paved with freeform black slate. The furnishings were a mix of antiques and contemporary pieces, and I remember that the living room sofa was covered in a warm celadon fabric and trimmed with trapunto, which was pretty unusual. If you grow up in surroundings like that, what else but decorating are you going to pursue as a career?

I didn't go to design school, though; I majored in business, largely because my father said I needed a job that would support me. Design, however, was an important part of how I saw the world, so much so that when I was eleven years old, my stepmother was having a patterned wallpaper installed in my father's and her bedroom, and I took one look and knew that something was wrong. "It's upside down," I said. She didn't believe me, so I got on my bicycle and pedaled down to the Sinclair paint store and brought home a wallpaper sample book to prove it. Well, that was the beginning of something. By the time I was twenty, when I didn't think I knew anything, friends of my parents from their ballroom-dancing group were asking my advice about drapery fabric and wallpaper and paint. They must have seen something in me, some sort of talent or taste, and off I went, into design, by the seat of my pants. I had to learn how to draw on a quarter-inch scale, so my father taught me. Then I practiced furniture plans, sketched layouts, and got a resale number. Decorating just felt right to me.

After more than forty years, most of them as head of my own interiors business, design still feels right. It's like a calling; I can't imagine doing anything else. Nothing excites me more than hearing from a client who has just bought a home with a certain pedigree and wants me to restore or renovate it, or working with an architect on building a house from

INTRODUCTION

the ground up. One day I'm developing a Francophile interior, another day I'm designing a contemporary residence with all custom furnishings, and on yet another day I find myself planning a ranch house in the wine country where the clients and I have shopped in Europe for antiques with patina and are mixing in exceptional contemporary paintings and sculpture.

As my clients have become more successful, their minds have opened and their trust in me has deepened, which allows me and my staff and the artisans and craftspeople who have worked with us for so long to create outside the box, often way outside. A living room sofa built around a towering lamp that spreads out like the branches of a tree? We've done that. A powder room paneled in a mosaic of onyx backlit so that the stone glows from within? We've done that, too, along with custom-made kitchen cabinets that are strapped with patinated brass and brushed stainless steel and paired with lava-rock counters. There's absolutely nothing you can't dream up for a design project, and, trust me, we've explored a lot of possibilities.

Having a particular look is something I've never wanted in my work. I haven't consciously avoided having one since I went into business for myself in the 1980s, it's just that, for me, every project is something new and requires a different perspective. Even when the clients are the same, they often want a fresh challenge, and I'm all about challenges, which is probably why I enjoy my work so much. Each new assignment gives me a chance to create spaces that don't look like anything I've done before.

During the course of my four-decade career, I have designed four, five, and even more houses for the same client, from city to country, beach to mountain, and everything in between. Each of those homes reflects its owner's personality, which is one reason I wanted to write this book: to share my process, to explain the relationships that I have with antiques dealers and craftspeople, to navigate the interactions between clients and myself, and, often, those between husband and wife as I wait for a decision to be made.

Also, the book gives me the chance to make it clear that art is essential to every interior. Art is hugely important to me, but the paintings and sculptures don't have to be by important artists. I love the work of regional artists as much as I do that of internationally famous ones. One of the elements of decorating that makes me the happiest is when I have been able to help clients understand how crucial art is in putting their stamp on their rooms and then introduce them to gallerists and art consultants I trust and whose taste I think the clients would appreciate. After that, I tend to step aside, because selecting art should be entirely personal. I'll figure out the best places to display the paintings and position the sculptures, but the collections should have nothing to do with me and everything to do with the clients. This is really what the best decorating is all about: an end result specific to a person or a couple or a family. I am fortunate enough to bring it all together.

RARE VINTAGE

ART AND ANTIQUES ON ALEXANDER'S CROWN

Think of a geographic location and certain clichés always come to mind: blue and white or seashells and beige by the seashore, stone and timber in the mountains. But when long-time clients of mine with homes in San Francisco and Laguna Beach purchased acres atop Alexander's Crown in Healdsburg, California, in the wine country of Sonoma County, and commissioned architect Howard Backen, with his associate Kirby Lee, to build them a very long, very handsome house where hearty beams cross vaulted ceilings and the huge windows are elegant grids of metal and glass, the wife made it clear that no cute traditions would be tolerated. No wine barrels, and absolutely no grape motifs. Instead, she told me that she wanted an individual décor: interesting, approachable, and comfortable, and with plenty of diversions, like a bocce court and a two-story "Treehouse" for guests.

The main house has incredible scale and volumes, with doors and windows ten feet tall, including the sliding entrance doors of quilted metal. The footprint of the house is big, but it is modest in how it sits on the land, camouflaged by old olive trees. The windows face west and east, so every room has two perspectives, taking in views of scrub, vineyards, and the Russian River. Working with architects from the start of every project is crucial to me in developing the right detailing and materials, and here, in collaboration with Kirby Lee, that resulted in, among other things, beams and floors made from reclaimed French oak planks to create an organic harmony within the architecture's hard-edged envelope. As for the interior decoration, it's an easygoing blend that I can only describe as contemporary: a mix of silhouettes, textures, and materials, where modern furniture meets antiques and vintage pieces, as well as custom-made furnishings and lots of one-off light fixtures.

Making every house an individual statement is a challenge I greatly enjoy, coming up with designs and solutions that are created specifically for one project and that won't be repeated for anyone else. The pair of lights on the breakfast table, for example, are two antique spheres, one a globe, the other the signs of the zodiac, for which an artisan house that I have worked with for more than three decades, Paul Ferrante Inc., made bases so we could turn them into lamps. The dramatically angled marble sink in the powder room I drew on a napkin, inspired by an old-fashioned washboard; the water trickles down the ribbed slope to the basin. My goal is always to put a great deal of thought into every component and juxtaposition in a house, but not to have it look overwrought. Here, the rooms feel destined to my mind, an interior complement to the garden design by Claudia Schmidt, where every plant and every tree looks as if it were always meant to be there. So does the art, from a striped Sol LeWitt to an edgy George Condo portrait to a small marble sculpture shaped like a stylized owl. Paintings and sculptures add an important dimension to an interior, and since art is a very personal decision, I always encourage my clients to develop a relationship with an art consultant or gallerist to figure out what they like and how it will fit into their lives.

The very first thing the clients and I purchased for the house was a massive and striking cryptomeria wood carving of a toad for the entry hall. The wife is Japanese, and in Japan, the frog (*kaeru*) is a symbol of good luck and prosperity, so I took that idea and had frog finials made for the bed in the primary bedroom. She likes red, too, so that color shows up frequently. We ended up taking three shopping trips to Europe together, primarily Belgium, France, and England, as well as one to Round Top, that Texas antiques mecca, looking for anything unique, anything unusual. In Belgium, we found huge citrus-crate planters from Spain that we grouped together by the front door. We liked the way they looked and bought a total of ten, having them lined so that we could use them on the property. An antiquarian friend of a friend joined us on one of the trips abroad, and he got us into jam-packed and very obscure barns and warehouses, where we could take our time, picking and choosing and spotting objects that we knew could be inventively repurposed. A pair of antique doors wound up becoming a headboard in one bedroom, while another headboard is fashioned from a wonderful old gate. The client spotted some green-painted doors that she didn't purchase, though they did inspire the green paint that brightens the pantry. A magnificent vintage steel table in the primary kitchen was originally from the Banque de France, and the living room's Lanvin cocktail table we found in the Paris flea market. We all agreed that it was incredibly cool, with a great shape, but it was too glossy. So I took off the shine and made it matte.

Silhouettes and contours are just as important as materials and colors, and the best arrangements are conversations in three dimensions: soft relating to solid, curved reacting to straight, rough responding to refined. The right blend makes for a lively décor, though not every choice is appreciated—at least, not right away. The big curved sofa in the family room didn't impress the wife at first, but the shape won her over. She says that it makes her feel as if it is putting its arms around her. Which is why it's the most popular seat in the room, the spot where she and her husband sit together, watch movies, and have some good wine. Breaking out a nice red at the end of the day is probably the only clichéd moment in a house specifically designed to avoid them, but it's one that's entirely appropriate.

PAGES 16–17: Sliding doors open to reveal a grand entry hall, anchored by a nineteenth-century Italian saddle-work table and huge citrus-crate planters we found in Belgium. The dog sculpture is from Formations.

PAGE 18: The house sits atop Alexander's Crown in Healdsburg, overlooking the most fully planted wine region in Sonoma County.

PAGE 21: Off the entry corridor is a space that leads to the living room, crowned by a plaster handkerchief pendant that was made in Paris and featuring an antique carpet from Woven. The console at left was found at Therien, and Swiss icon Willy Guhl designed the wasp-waist, white cement planter in the 1970s.

PRECEDING PAGES: A Beatriz Milhazes painting surveys the living room, where the lighting includes a custom Paul Ferrante chandelier with shades made from antique French linen. Upholstered in a custom-colored Rosemary Hallgarten alpaca bouclé, the custom-made Harte Davis sofa is joined by a François-Xavier Lalanne sheep. A trip to the Paris flea market turned up the vintage Arne Jacobsen egg chair.

RIGHT: Another view of the living room, surfaced with Venetian plaster, illustrates how the vaulted space is framed by sliding doors and portières. The perforated white end table was found at the Paris flea market, and the limited-edition Gemini cocktail table, with a rock-crystal surface supported by bronze-finish aluminum legs, was designed by fashion house scion Jean-Yves Lanvin.

OVERLEAF LEFT: Another custom Paul Ferrante chandelier with shades made of antique French linen is suspended above a dining table that a Belgian shop made for us using an industrial base from France. The custom-made chairs were inspired by a vintage Scandinavian design.

OVERLEAF RIGHT: In the working kitchen, known as the pantry or cook's kitchen, the custom-made cabinets are surfaced in a green finish inspired by sun-bleached antique shutters that were spotted during a European buying trip. Quartzite with a hand-applied organic finish was used for the counters, and the faucets are from Watermark.

RIGHT: The custom furniture atelier Paul Ferrante Inc. created a pair of dramatic tall table lamps for the primary kitchen, combining custom-made metal bases with vintage globes, one a map of the world and the other the signs of the zodiac. The vintage table, purchased at the Paris flea market, was originally made for the Banque de France; it is surrounded by Thomas Hayes barstools and two Sempione stools by Natasha Baradaran.

OVERLEAF LEFT: A sinuous Coup D'Etat sofa makes a sculptural statement in the family room, as do a pair of low Martini chairs by Willam (Billy) Haines, which are dressed in a Pierre Frey fabric. The custom-made fireplace was designed to look like recycled I-beams, and the custom-made ceiling fixture is a Paul Ferrante creation.

OVERLEAF RIGHT: In a sunny, stone-floored space known as the terrace, a rugged Formations table is surrounded by Sutherland armchairs with cushions covered in a Perennials woven stripe.

PAGE 32: In a corridor that links the wine cellar to the party room, a graphic portrait by American artist George Condo spans one Venetian-plastered wall. The sculpture on the wall to the left is by William Kentridge.

PAGE 33: The custom-designed wine cellar is encased in glass and bronze.

OPPOSITE: Frogs top the posts of the primary bedroom's custom-made iron bed, which is flanked by vintage nightstands from Lee Stanton. A Zak+Fox fabric covers the headboard and footboard, and Barbara Martin linens dress the bed. The green wool Indian throw is from One Fine Nest. The antique carpet is from Woven.

ABOVE: Custom-made cabinets line the primary bath, where the Drummonds tub stands on a floor paved with turtle-patterned quartzite from Concept Studio.

LEFT: Harte designed the powder room's hand-aged French limestone sink after old-fashioned washboards: the water ripples, from left to right, down a ribbed surface. The walls are upholstered in linen with steel bands, and the sconces in the shape of hands were custom-made by Paul Ferrante.

OPPOSITE: A Sol LeWitt artwork hangs above an antique French console from Galerie Half.

RIGHT: A guest room features a Thomas Hayes bed and a pair of curtained alcove beds. The vintage carpet is from Woven, the Banque de France steel writing desk was found in Paris, and the light fixtures are by Urban Electric Company.

OVERLEAF: In the lounge, a solution-dyed Perennials carpet hosts an Eleanor Rigby Home sofa, Egyptian-plaster tripod occasional tables by John Dickinson, a rush-and-wood Orkney chair, and custom-made Harte Davis blue-sheepskin-covered ottomans. The industrial-style metal ceiling fixtures are actually old French factory lights.

PAGES 42–43: The clients enjoy hosting, and as we planned the indoor-outdoor flow of the home, we designed the lounge to open onto the pool.

PRECEDING PAGES: In addition to an outdoor dining area and a spacious pool deck, a pair of Ledge Lounger chaises set in the pool offer a relaxing perch to take in the surrounding landscape.

LEFT: Known as the Treehouse, an ancillary building on the property serves as accommodation for guests.

OVERLEAF LEFT: Tiles inspired by antique English encaustic tiles were used to create a colorful patchwork floor in a Treehouse bathroom. The antique-seeming sink is by Kohler.

OVERLEAF RIGHT: Harte designed the headboard for the Treehouse bed from an antique stable gate found in Europe. A Ralph Lauren fabric cushions the vintage armchairs, and the carpet is from Woven.

PAGES 48–49: The property's bocce court is a familial gathering spot, with a pair of vintage Willy Guhl chairs at one end and a group of Adirondack chairs from Sutherland Furniture.

SENSUAL
SURFACES

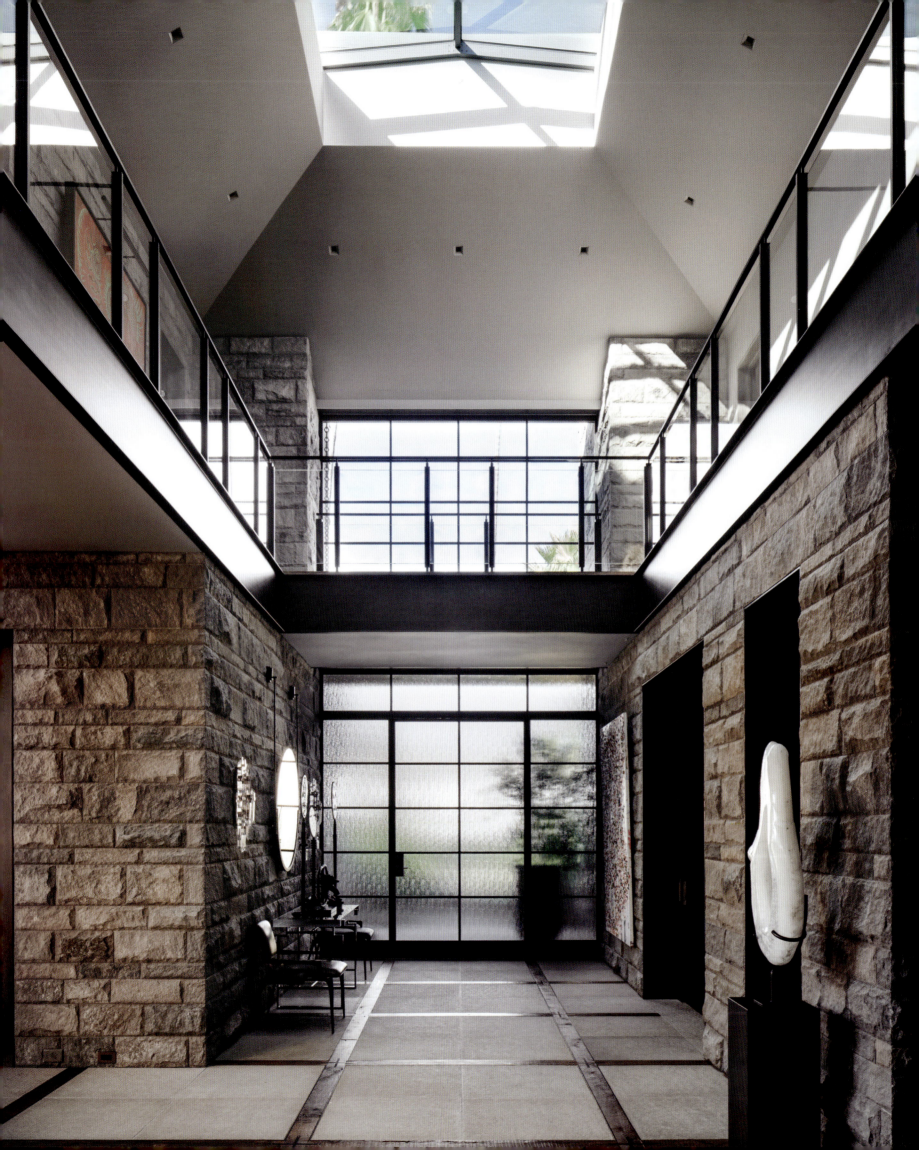

RUSTIC TEXTURES WOVEN WITH MODERN SENSIBILITIES

Change is not only good, sometimes it's the option you hope for. I had decorated seven houses for one of my clients, in locations ranging from Deer Valley, Utah, to Orange County, California. The earlier houses were conceived in her favorite Mediterranean Revival style, with a palette of mustard yellows and olive greens. Then, one day, she bought some land in the flats of Beverly Hills and asked architect Richard Landry to design a new house. This time around, she came to me with a surprisingly modern vision of gray, taupe, and black. She wanted more contemporary furnishings, more sensual surfaces, and lots of textures. It was totally different from what she had been living with for so long, and I was excited to take on this challenge with her. She used the term *modern farmhouse*, which did not sit well with me in this context, but I gave her the spirit of what she wanted, in terms of the color schemes.

Landry designed a very contemporary house but with a traditional character, like a house in Belgium that has been crossed with a barn, yet there's nothing rural about it. The interiors, on the other hand, are composed of modern elements mixed with a lot of textures and opposites-attract moments, like the looping crystal chandelier in the dining room that hangs above a graphic floor of reclaimed French oak planks arranged into concentric squares. Elsewhere, there are earthy but sophisticated juxtapositions of stone, mirror, and metal, such as the stone floor in the entrance hall, which is crisscrossed with wood and speckled with brass crosses, and a bar that is wrapped in a dark smoky quartz. The kitchen cabinets are faced with heavily wire-brushed oak that has been strapped with bands of stainless steel and brass, a bit like a Rolex watch; the counters are made of custom lava stone. Every reclining seat in the home cinema is cushioned with natural sheepskin, just one of many soft, velvety textures that offset the building's emphasis on hard materials. The whole house has a smoky atmosphere, somewhat moody yet very serene, with misty colors. The rooms are very comfortable, though, with furniture you want to sink into.

The views are a big part of the experience, too, and they—and the landscaping—affected the composition of each space. As with any house in which the windows are large enough to frame substantial aspects of the property, I had to consider the amount of light that pours in or, conversely, the amount of shade that's cast. I also had to take into account the weather patterns and whether a room accesses the outside or not. An interior designer works from the inside out, while an architect works from the outside in. The dining room, for example, gets a lot of natural light, but the family room has a more shadowy feeling, which gave me the idea to incorporate a coffee table with a metallic finish that adds some shimmer and shine. A similar combination of materials and tones shows up in the breakfast room, which has not one table but two, because the client enjoys playing mahjong with her friends. And if the women want to dine, the tables can be pushed together. The chandelier in that space is pretty extraordinary, and as with most of the light fixtures in the house, we tapped into our well of inspiration and collaborated on a design that was handmade by the Paul Ferrante artisan house.

Like all my projects, there are tons of custom elements, from furniture to surfaces. The powder room is paneled with custom polished white agate slabs outlined in gold, and concealed lighting accents the living room's stepped chimneypiece and ceiling. I also wanted to do something different and striking, more sculptural than usual, for the primary bedroom: the headboard is composed of two side-by-side sections that are channel-quilted at different levels. The channels don't connect, but I like that. One of the biggest challenges was how to treat the main staircase. The client likes custom carpeting, so we had the runner woven in Tibet, China, and the pattern had to fit seamlessly from tread to tread, up two flights, with the knowledge that each tread is a separate piece and there is a gap between each one. Completing that commission was quite a feat, creatively and mathematically, but it all lined up.

The overall effect is just what the client hoped for: a subdued palette sparked by colorful contemporary art by the likes of George Condo and Damien Hirst; the combination of custom and artisan furnishings and lighting; and a pleasing balance of hard and soft, smooth and rugged, clean-lined and sensual. It's certainly not a modern farmhouse, though. As I told her, show me one farmer who has ever lived like this.

PAGES 50–51: A Damien Hirst painting is reflected in the entrance hall's mirror, the form of which is echoed in several Feliciano Béjar sculptures created from vintage car parts. The table is a Paul Ferrante design, the sconce (one of a pair) is from Wired, and the floor is an oversized grid of stone, brass, and wood.

PRECEDING PAGES: A skylight running the entire length of the entrance hall warms the interior stone and metal surfaces, as do the strips of wood crisscrossing the stone floor.

OPPOSITE: Instead of closing in the stairway off the living room and bar, we designed a retro-style openwork brass screen for a touch of glam.

RIGHT: A George Condo painting is mounted on one wall of the living room, where concealed lighting defines the space. The custom-made Harte Davis sofa is clad in a Rosemary Hallgarten alpaca with leather cording, and the Paul Ferrante chairs are cushioned with a hand-patinated leather.

RIGHT: Concealed lighting stripes the brushed Magic Brown marble fireplace in the living room, where Coup D'Etat swivel chairs nestle near the hearth. Embroidery Palace stitched the decorative details on the wool-sateen draperies, and the cocktail table is a custom Harte Davis design.

LEFT: The exposed concrete ceiling with suspended LED lighting and walls upholstered in a moody JAB tweed give the lounge a modern, masculine vibe. Nathan Anthony sectionals rest on a hand-woven wool rug from Woven, and the custom coffee tables feature leather bumpers.

RIGHT: In the dining room, an infinity chandelier makes a sharp contrast to the reclaimed French oak floor. The A. Rudin chairs are covered in a Lauren Hwang fabric, and the windows are draped with custom-made Rosemary Hallgarten sheers. The fireplace, made of petrified wood, is set within a framework of cold-rolled steel, and the table is custom Harte Davis.

BELOW AND OPPOSITE: A Paul Ferrante light fixture hangs above a bar sheathed in a smoky quartz. The bar itself is fashioned of wire-brushed oak, antiqued mirror, and custom-made brass screens.

RIGHT: In the kitchen, Thomas Hayes barstools gather at the island, which is made of hand-distressed black Petit Granit, a Belgian limestone. The island's lower cabinets are ebonized oak, while the peripheral cabinets are scrubbed oak topped with custom lava stone.

OVERLEAF LEFT: Belgian Petit Granit was used for the counters in the butler's pantry. The lower cabinets are made of ebonized oak, and the upper cabinets of antiqued brass with a brushed finish.

OVERLEAF RIGHT: The kitchen range is by Wolf, the custom-designed hood features brass studs, and the backsplash is lined with custom-made zinc panels.

PAGES 70–71: The family area is anchored by a custom-made A. Rudin sectional sofa covered in a Rosemary Hallgarten bouclé. The hair-on-hide chairs also are a Harte Davis design, the metal-clad cocktail tables are by Gentner, and the carpet is from Woven.

BELOW AND OPPOSITE: Trimmed with antiqued brass, a machine-patterned black limestone from Concept Studio textures the walls of the home office. The angular desk is by Scala Luxury, the armchair and ottoman are from Minotti, and the carpet is from Erik Lindström. Shimmering panels from Phillip Jeffries line the coffered ceiling.

OVERLEAF: Softened by a custom-made runner that was woven in Tibet, China, the staircase rises above a sand garden where, combining evocativeness and practicality, a preserved bonsai tree is a featured element.

OPPOSITE: Custom polished white agate slabs outlined in gold line a wall in the powder room, which is further illuminated by custom-made Paul Ferrante pendants. The chair, from Therien, is upholstered in angora.

BELOW: A Damien Hirst painting enlivens the stairway, where the runner's crisscross motif is echoed in the Wired light fixture.

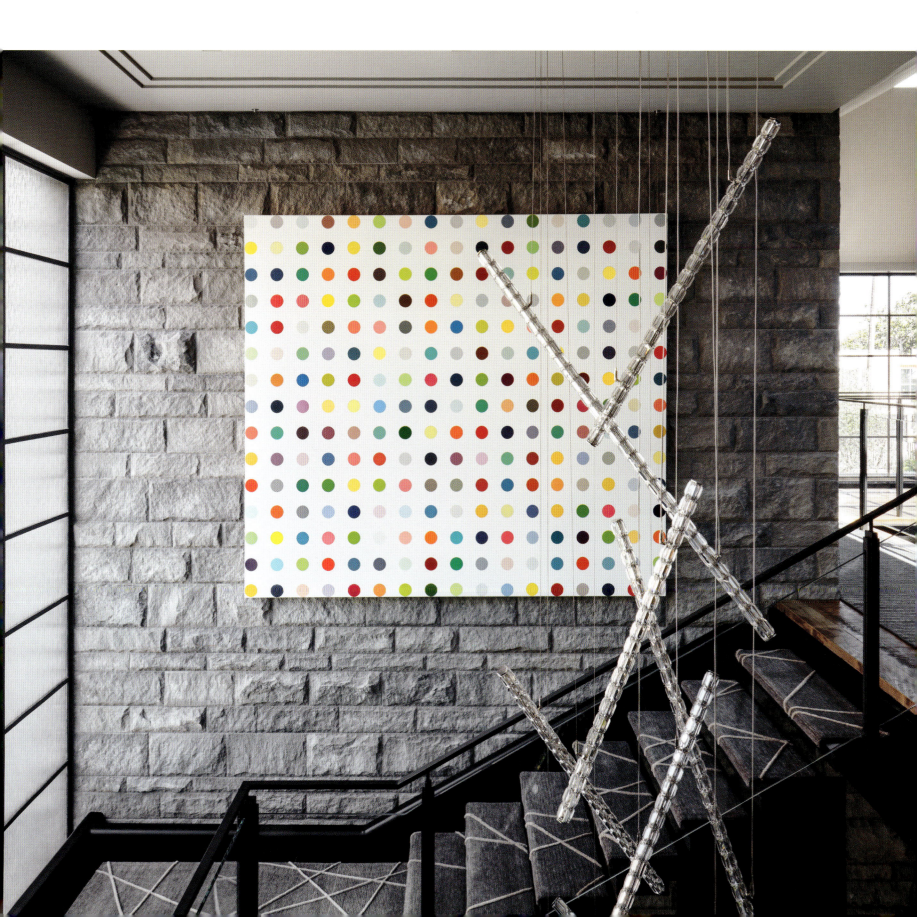

RIGHT: In the primary bedroom, Larose Guyon's Céleste chandelier, made of a hundred aged-brass jewelry chains, floats above an array of sensuous textures, including Fortuny bedding, a sheepskin-covered bench, and an alpaca throw pillow. I deliberately didn't match up the two sections of the channel-quilted headboard to draw attention to it.

OVERLEAF LEFT: A dramatic vault of reclaimed French oak shelters the primary bathroom, which is paneled in the same material.

OVERLEAF RIGHT: A wainscot of polished silver cristallo quartzite wraps the space, which is lit by a combination of Apparatus fixtures and recessed lighting. A Drummonds tub stands in a recess.

RIGHT: Boulders break up the pool's rectilinear silhouette and add a note of ruggedness, as if the pool were constructed around natural outcroppings. Formations' Polyhedron side tables blend right in. The chaises are also from Formations, and the umbrella is by Sutherland.

OVERLEAF: Beneath the pergola, the zinc-topped teak farm table is from Petersen. The Bernhardt Santa Cruz armchairs feature an all-weather, soft-knit sock weave wrapped around an aluminum frame.

PAGES 86–87: Formations chaises cushioned in Perennials fabrics are shaded by a Sutherland Furniture umbrella.

PAGES 88–89: Cypresses tower above a lyrical Kevin Robb sculpture that punctuates the pool area.

THE SHAPE OF HOME

THESE ARE SOME HIGH-END GAYS

PALM SPRINGS / OLD LAS PALMAS, CALIFORNIA |

One of my biggest gifts as a designer is also one of my most dangerous weaknesses as a homeowner: I welcome any challenge. That's how my husband, John, and I came to undertake the exhaustive overhaul of a 1941 Spanish-style bungalow in the Old Las Palmas neighborhood of Palm Springs. It was one of my most transformative and, of course, most deeply personal projects.

John and I had been coming to Palm Springs for many years and had owned several homes in different neighborhoods, but we'd always coveted Old Las Palmas. The streets are lined in an enticing mix of Spanish Colonial and midcentury-modern homes, a veritable time capsule of the area's architectural development in the 1920s and subsequent expansion during Palm Springs' heyday in the mid-twentieth century, when Hollywood descended on the desert locale because it was situated just inside the 100-mile radius that studios mandated for their contracted stars' homes.

When I walked into the house for the first time, I told John, "It looks like two old ladies lived here." It had no panache. Instead of taking maximum advantage of Palm Springs' vaunted sunny climate and indoor-outdoor lifestyle, the interior was dark and enclosed. Whereas its Spanish style called for textural finishes and bold silhouettes, it had a drab color scheme and dated materials, even though, surprisingly, it had been remodeled two years before we saw it. But as a designer with four decades of experience, I visualized the possibilities immediately—and we bought it on the spot.

The first step was to bring more natural light into the house and open it to the mountain views. I removed a narrow interior hallway, relocated the living room fireplace, which had occupied the center of the space, to one end of the room, and opened the dining room to the living room with a wide archway. I blew out solid walls and replaced them with glass: a fourteen-foot-long slider in the living room and steel-framed French doors in the primary bedroom now overlook the courtyard pool area and offer stunning views of the desert landscape and mountains beyond.

I love a black-and-white palette, and here it served as the perfect scheme to showcase the sculptural nature of the new interior architecture. I stained the ceiling beams a dark color that looks modern but is also in keeping with the original Spanish style. White plaster walls are offset by the beams and the black Petit Granit floors, which we finished with white grout for high contrast. In my childhood home, my mother, who had wonderful taste, had installed black slate floors, and I've loved the look of them ever since.

Against this graphic backdrop, our curated mix of art, furniture, and objects can really sing. I've spent decades building relationships with trusted vendors, artists, and artisans, and John and I have a habit of buying things we love and finding a place for them, so nearly every piece in the home has a story to tell. In the living room, furniture I bought on a shopping trip with my good friend Lee Stanton is paired with items from the estate of a late friend of John; the Native American sculptural figure on our kitchen island was purchased on John's and my first trip together.

We enlisted my foster brother, decorative painter Robert O'Neil, to hand-paint several rooms in the house: a graphic, black-and-white mural for one guest room and a sepia-toned mural for our bedroom. He also translated a wonky idea into a wholly unique scheme for our powder room, emblazoning the walls and ceiling with maxims from John's and my families, ranging from the endearing ("Home is where you get your emotional groceries") to the amusing ("Balls, balls, cried the queen. If I had two, I'd be the king"). And one that my design friends enjoy: "Oh that person, they're a bulb short of a chandelier."

John's one request was to bring more color into the house, so I layered in reds, oranges, blues, and greens in the form of rugs and pillows in the living room and infused our bedroom with accents of cerulean. We went all out in the guest rooms; I covered the walls of one in a bold take on toile de Jouy by Pierre Frey. I relish the irreverence of the graffiti-style markings over the traditional pattern, which I paired with graphic, black-and-white-striped

PAGES 90-91: In the entry, in front of a still life by Raimonds Staprans, a vintage workbench holds a chain sculpture bought on a trip to Sonoma and a Willy Guhl vase—a hint of the dramatic silhouettes in the spaces beyond.

PAGES 92-93: Black Petit Granit floors and dark ceiling beams add contrast to the open, airy living space created from a series of interconnected rooms. A lovingly curated mix of vintage, antique, and contemporary furnishings is punctuated by an ever-revolving mix of art, including a bronze totem by Rod Kagan and Roger Kuntz's *Pavement Arrow*. Topping the room is Larry Bell's *Light Knot* kinetic sculpture, exhibited at the Whitney Museum in 2015.

PRECEDING PAGES: In the family room off the kitchen, textural elements like the rough-hewn coffee table, the vintage buffet, and the sofa upholstered in a Pierre Frey bouclé imbue a sense of comfort. The painting is by Jimi Gleason, the rustic buffet, which conceals a television lift, is from Obsolete, and the chair is from Phlip Stites.

OPPOSITE: In the dining area, which is separated from the living space by a wide, arched opening, a Paul Ferrante chandelier spotlights the Robert Kuo repoussé tree-trunk table with white lacquer top and early 1900s Scandinavian armchairs with the original leather, from antiquarian Lee Stanton. Tony DeLap's painting *Hat Trick* was a gift from John.

bedding and window shades. In the other, fringed green draperies (made from Indian bedspreads) pop against Robert's black-and-white mural; an Élitis emerald-and-black wallpaper of totem poles, emulating desert cacti, continues this scheme in the adjoining bath.

Art is extremely important to us, and that's one element of our house that is always changing. John and I keep adding new items to our collection, and I tend to move things around, rotating what we look at the most. Right now, Roger Kuntz's *Pavement Arrow* hangs in the living room between the twin arched doorways leading to the entryway; next week it might be a metal sculpture. I like putting different pieces in conversation with each other too: the juxtaposition of a bronze totem by Rod Kagan and Kuntz's painting brings a certain dynamism to the living room.

Outside, I reimagined the landscape with my dear friend and landscape designer the late Marcello Villano. We re-clad the pool and spa in Moroccan tile and replaced the terrace with warm stone that complements the textural plaster of the house. An exterior fireplace extends the outdoor season and creates an interesting focal point at one end of the courtyard. To further ground the space, we craned in two large olive trees to anchor the front wall and provide much-needed shade. In the back, we installed an outdoor dining area with a pizza oven off the kitchen, then turned what had once been a narrow strip of unused turf into an arcade, where strategic planting and exterior art make for compelling sightlines from inside.

Although this home is our shared getaway, John was very hands-off in the process. He entrusted it completely to me and encouraged me to realize my vision, which may be the best gift the spouse of a creative can bestow. As a result, I got to present the house to John as I would to a client, which made it feel like a gift from me to him. And though in many ways this was a house for John, it's also become a home for everyone we love. Our guest rooms are full nearly every weekend during the season, and everybody who stays here cherishes the experience. And that, I think, is the true measure of a great home.

BELOW: A custom backsplash from Concept Studio creates a zippy pattern in the kitchen. The reclaimed-oak island is topped with white organic quartzite and lit with pendants by Lindsey Adelman. Leather-topped barstools from Blackman Cruz create a casual eating area.

RIGHT: A sleek chrome-and-leather bed—a gift from a client—contrasts with the plush rug from Woven and the Romo shearling–covered daybed in the primary bedroom, which opens onto a secluded patio. The blue, espresso, and white bedding echoes the colors of the Scot Heywood canvas behind.

BELOW: In the Green Bedroom, named for the draperies made from Indian bedspreads, a custom mural by Robert O'Neil continues the home's black-and-white scheme. A wood-and-leather bed from Thomas Hayes Studio faces the pool outside.

OPPOSITE: In the adjacent bathroom, an Élitis wallpaper, an artwork by Cecil Touchon, and tiles by Concept Studio continue the Green Bedroom's color scheme.

LEFT: In the Red Bedroom, a metallic canvas by Jimi Gleason and a Hunt Slonem bunny painting are an unusual pairing atop a bold, irreverent toile de Jouy wallpaper by Pierre Frey. The Paul Ferrante chandelier is one of several throughout the house.

105

LEFT: The addition of a custom-designed, Spanish-style outdoor fireplace creates a focal point at the end of the pool area. It provides a cozy gathering space for chilly Palm Springs evenings. The coffee tables are antique.

OVERLEAF: Two mature olive trees flanking the pool deck add height to the landscape. The hammered-iron outdoor furniture is from Formations; the cushions are covered in an InsideOut fabric.

MID-CENTURY DREAM

VINTAGE GLAMOUR IN RANCHO MIRAGE

The Hollywood film industry turned the desert, as the Palm Springs area is known, into a glamorous locale in the 1950s. Parties poolside under swaying palm trees extended from day to night, and bowties and long dresses were de rigueur. One of my longtime clients has a reverence for that Rat Pack era, and, of all the projects I've completed in the desert, from Palm Springs to Indian Wells, this one comes closest to the aesthetic of that time.

The house, completed in 1957, sits on a plot in the storied Thunderbird Country Club, where the likes of Bob Hope, Bing Crosby, and Desi Arnaz rubbed shoulders with leaders in politics and business (including auto execs from Detroit, who adopted the club name for the famous Ford sports car), enjoyed Palm Springs' first eighteen-hole golf course, and commissioned many modern homes.

It's easy to see why this client, a history buff with a keen sense of design, understood the appeal of this particular slice of the California desert. When he first laid eyes on the house, though, that appeal wasn't readily apparent. As a true period home that had been poorly updated since its midcentury completion, it was stuffed with furniture and fixtures that were more passé than mod. But eventually, the potential inherent in its modern structure prevailed, and we began the careful process of restoring the home to its former glory.

Our first task was to pare the home back, stripping it of unnecessary detail—and décor—to reveal terrazzo floors, warm stonework, and expansive mountain views through wide windows. Taking our cues from this foundation, we revived the architectural shell for modern living. To keep the focus on the architecture, I looked to period-appropriate materials that introduced understated warmth. We extended the terrazzo floors throughout the house, covered the walls in Venetian plaster, and clad the ceilings in cedar panels, which lent both warmth and subtle texture—as did the use of more textural woods such as olive and eucalyptus as accents. And in a nod to the industrial aesthetic of midcentury modernism, we incorporated stainless-steel trim and detailing.

This cleaned-up vision of period design drove the furniture plan too. The client has a deep appreciation for *good* midcentury furniture and great taste in art (the home contains work by the likes of Alexander Calder, Frank Gehry, and Charles Arnoldi), and the house presented the perfect opportunity to marry the two. We outfitted the open living and dining area with midcentury icons in warm, neutral colors that echo the interior architecture: white leather Barcelona chairs with stainless-steel legs, low-slung Billy Haines sofas arranged back-to-back, an elegant Arco floor lamp by Achille and Pier Giacomo Castiglioni and a more sculptural floor lamp by Dragonette, an Eero Saarinen marble-topped pedestal table and matching Tulip chairs with their famous Space Age burnt-orange cushions.

The more enclosed spaces became canvases for daring materials, bolder patterns, and richer hues, like a powder room wallcovering embossed with a crocodile pattern, a pair of swivel chairs upholstered in a pink Pucci print, and a graphic graphite-and-ivory Kelly Wearstler wallpaper swathing a guest room.

As with all the best midcentury-modern architecture—especially in the Palm Springs climate—the house is in constant dialogue with its landscape, the design of which was a collaboration with the late Marcello Villano. Together, we streamlined the exterior architecture, extended interior materials to the outdoors, and designed an organic landscape of textural, indigenous vegetation.

Around the refinished pool, I continued the line of the house's roof overhang in the form of a modern pergola designed by Marcello to shelter an outdoor dining area, drawing the flow of the house outward. Now, whether seated in the living room's sofas or outdoors on the pool deck, it's hard to tell where the interior ends and the exterior begins—especially when the sliding glass doors are open to the fresh air. And isn't that the very best version of indoor-outdoor living?

PAGES 110–11: In a corner of the primary bedroom, vintage midcentury swivel chairs with their original, vibrant Pucci-print upholstery nod to the home's modernist pedigree.

PRECEDING PAGES: A graphic canvas by Kim MacConnel offsets the warm wood paneling and sleek terrazzo floors in the front hallway; the Holly Hunt bench is a contemporary interpretation of the midcentury silhouettes throughout the home.

OPPOSITE: In a departure from painted walls, Venetian plaster with a finish emulating polished concrete frames the view of the pool and palm trees beyond.

OVERLEAF: Under a cedar-paneled ceiling in the living area, midcentury classics like back-to-back Billy Haines sofas, a chrome Arco floor lamp by Achille and Pier Giacomo Castiglioni, Mies van der Rohe Barcelona chairs, and a Hans Wegner walnut Shell chair share space with contemporary designs. Embroidered pillows by Jennifer Robbins add a hint of pattern.

PRECEDING PAGES LEFT: Preserving the home's original stone fireplace surround was important to the historically minded client. A custom coffee table by Joseph Jeup and a Dragonette floor lamp bring a contemporary flair to the space, clearly a favorite of bulldog Louie.

PRECEDING PAGES RIGHT: Sculptural white leather chairs surround a monumental white table in the dining area. The all-white furniture lets the bold artwork and brass-fronted sideboard from Scala Luxury sing. The light fixture is vintage.

OPPOSITE: In the breakfast area, a Martin Snipper painting overlooks an Eero Saarinen Tulip table and matching dining chairs with iconic burnt-orange cushions. The sculptural Artemide light fixture provides visual interest without detracting from the clean lines of the space.

OVERLEAF LEFT: Closets in the primary suite are concealed by sliding parchment panels custom-made by Shoji, a Japanese company in Los Angeles.

OVERLEAF RIGHT: A grouping of drawings by Frank Gehry against a graphic wallpaper by Kelly Wearstler and a custom headboard upholstered in a Groundworks fabric create a play of patterns in the guest room.

PAGES 124-25: The essence of midcentury modern: the home's interior spaces spill out to the exterior, where a poolside living area, dining space, and kitchen and bar invite alfresco entertaining.

BREAKING WITH TRADITION

TAKE A WALK ON THE WILD SIDE

INDIAN WELLS / ELDORADO COUNTRY CLUB, CALIFORNIA

When longtime clients bought property in the desert, they visited our home in Palm Springs, looked around, and said, "We want a version of this—modern, with warmth and individuality." What better compliment could a designer get? This request, coupled with the clients' implicit trust, set the groundwork for a spectacular collaboration.

The house these clients bought is in Indian Wells at the iconic Eldorado Country Club—famously the first golf club with adjacent residences in the Palm Springs area. Fittingly, they are both big golfers and frequent hosts, with lots of friends and a big family who visit them often. The vision was to give them a comfortable, artful retreat where they could relax as a couple or host large gatherings.

This vision, however, seemed far off. The house they had purchased was a mid-1970s build that had suffered a succession of bad renovations that had transformed it into an eyesore, so we knew we had our work cut out for us. Working with interior architectural designer Donna Pozdro, we took the house completely down to the studs, stripping away any excess detailing and peeling back layers of finishes to create the foundation for an inviting, modern home with thoughtful layers and a good dose of drama.

Inside, the textures and patterns—teased by the pool's graphic, Moroccan-tile coping—came fully to life against the minimalist architecture. I knew the clients wanted a home that was modernist but not cold or stoic, and with their faith in the process, we were able to take risks with design and architecture that make for a singular expression of their vision.

One of the first things we did to warm up the place was to install reclaimed French oak planks on the floors throughout the house, giving an organic feel that offsets the graphic backdrop of white plaster walls and steel window frames. For the entry and bathroom floors, black Petit Granit continues the organic texture while sticking to a minimal palette.

We clad the fireplace and an existing built-in bar in oak paneling to give them fresh, new life and connect them to the oak cabinetry in the kitchen. As we often do, we drew every single detail in this house, and some of the seemingly smallest decisions made the biggest impact on the final project. The perfect example? My decision to include a half-inch-wide relief painted black along the ceilings and floors throughout the house added a subtle hint of depth and a continual graphic line that accentuates the linear architecture.

Surprisingly, a limited palette can sometimes elicit the most interestingly layered designs, and that was certainly the case in this house. In the dining room, we commissioned a custom black-and-white-and-gold-leaf wallpaper from Gracie in a dramatic, oversize pattern. Soaring, painterly gestures draw the eye up above the dining table, where we designed a custom light fixture with a brutalist feel. In the primary bedroom, swooping lines across the space look like graphite on parchment—an appropriate motif for art-collector clients. In one of the house's two guest casitas, a grayscale landscape by my foster brother, decorative artist Robert O'Neil, brings depth to the small space.

The graphic treatment continues in the bathrooms: in one, a matte-black soaking tub pops against luminescent, Moroccan-tile walls; in another, a dramatic slab vanity is paired with geometric, art deco–inspired waterjet patterns.

Texture was key in furnishing the public areas too: nubby bouclé on armchairs and bar-stools, shearling-upholstered dining chairs, and an organic linen on the modular Verellen sofa exude comfort; cushions in a tactile Fortuny fabric give antique garden chairs new life.

The restrained background palette meant that anyplace we used color was more dramatic, as in the entryway, where an abstract canvas by Charles Arnoldi packs a punch against the neutral backdrop. Leaning into the duality of the home's two casitas, we outfitted one in textural neutrals, in keeping with my foster brother's hand-painted grayscale mural, but went full-out maximalist in the other, cladding the bedroom in a tropical-hued Élitis wallpaper above colorful Clarence House pillows and the bathroom in Cole & Son's cheerful Arance pattern.

It's a thrill working with clients who let us take them on a design adventure.

PAGES 126–27: Black, white, and textural neutrals with a touch of glam were the vision for this house. The dining room's custom graphic Gracie wallpaper creates a dramatic backdrop for a sculptural, midcentury Russell Woodard chair outfitted with Fortuny cushions.

PRECEDING PAGES: Natural textures in the form of an antique wooden table and chairs from Lee Stanton, black marble lamps, a vintage zebra-skin rug, and a custom horsehair-fringed ottoman provide an organic contrast to the kaleidoscopic Charles Arnoldi painting. The antique wood floors are by Weaverbird, and the bust and antique cachepot are from Berbere Imports.

OPPOSITE: The living room walls are clad in custom oak paneling inset with horizontal bands that offset the wood's vertical grain. A suspended D'lisa Creager sculpture and sculptural armchairs by Arne Jacobsen and Fritz Hansen in leather and sheepskin, respectively, lend further texture to the space.

PAGES 132–33: With a palette limited to black, white, and neutrals, textures take center stage in the living room, where bouclé and sheepskin create intriguing depth. Pops of color come in the form of pillows covered in antique textiles from Pat McGann Gallery. The modular Verellen sofa not only has a modern, low-slung profile but is also multifunctional.

PRECEDING PAGES: An overscale, abstract-patterned wallpaper by Gracie has a dynamic effect in the dining room, where vintage Gianni Moscatelli dining chairs are upholstered in faux fur for maximum comfort. A custom metal light fixture has a brutalist feel.

OPPOSITE: Refitted with fresh oak cabinetry and a soaring mirror, the idiosyncratic sunken bar area has become a useful and inviting entertaining space.

ABOVE: In the kitchen, the zellige-tile backsplash has a luminescent effect under oak cabinetry. Thomas Hayes stools upholstered in a rich, orange leather line the quartzite counter. The four-part pendant is from McEwen Lighting.

OPPOSITE: In the adjacent breakfast nook, an articulated Ferrante light fixture illuminates Robert Kuo's red lacquer cherries sculpture, a cheeky and unexpected centerpiece, and a swarm of butterflies by Paul Villinski has alighted on the walls.

PRECEDING PAGES: In the primary bedroom, a wallcovering by artist Douglas Glovaski for Area Environments featuring an overscale pattern of intersecting graphite arcs is the perfect foil to bedding in plush Sandra Jordan alpaca. An olivewood bench from Lee Stanton and an assortment of Iraqi kilim rugs bring warmth to the space. The brass-clad mahogany nightstands are by Scala Luxury.

RIGHT: A pair of antique British armchairs from Obsolete flanking a Dutch side table found at Lee Stanton create a cozy sitting area. The still life is by Norman Sunshine.

OVERLEAF LEFT: An antique Moroccan side table adds a graphic punch in the bathroom, where a matte-black soaking tub and iridescent wall tiles continue the monochromatic theme.

OVERLEAF RIGHT: A custom mural painted by Robert O'Neil lends an artful touch to one of the home's two casitas. A multi-light pendant from Flos hangs over the Gabby bed.

OPPOSITE: The second casita takes a maximalist turn with a jungly, color-saturated Élitis paper covering one wall. In front of it stands an elaborately carved wood chest. The enamel lamp is vintage.

BELOW: The exuberant style continues into the guest bath, which is wallpapered in Cole & Son's Arance pattern.

OVERLEAF: In what was once a tangle of overwrought water features and outdated landscaping, a streamlined pool with the graphic touch of Moroccan tile presents a thoroughly modern interpretation. The lounge chairs are from McKinnon and Harris, and the umbrellas are by Perennials.

JEWEL BOX IN THE SKY

FASHIONING A CONTEMPORARY APARTMENT

One of the greatest gifts of our profession is the chance we get to grow with our clients. This apartment is for a couple whose first home I designed eighteen years ago. Nearly two decades later, not only are they in a much different phase of life, but their knowledge and exposure have grown and deepened, which always makes for a wonderful collaborative process. What I love about this apartment is that it feels so different from the other homes I've done for the couple, including their primary residence in Laguna Beach. Sometimes, clients with multiple homes want the same kind of feel for each house, but when the opportunity arises to create a totally different environment, I'm ready, willing, and able.

The couple purchased this apartment in a well-known San Francisco building to serve as a pied-à-terre. The existing interiors were very traditional, and, while they wanted the bones to be somewhat classical in nature, they were keen to give the apartment a more chic, modern city feel—something with a bit of edge. They tapped principal Andrew Skurman and Suzette Smith, then an associate, of Skurman Architects, who had worked on multiple apartments in the building, to realize their vision of an urbane reinterpretation of the existing space. The wife has great personal style; she's not only very interested in fashion (she's a big Isabel Marant fan) but also a passionate art collector. She and I have a great synergy; we have a lot of fun bouncing things off each other, and this project gave us plenty of opportunity to do that.

Somewhat paradoxically, Skurman and Smith's knowledge of classical architecture and proportion was instrumental in developing a modern interpretation of this space. Instead of ignoring the classical architecture of the building, they built on it in creative ways, giving classical elements new functions: arches frame a headboard and a bathroom vanity, barrel-vaulted ceilings make the small entry and powder room appear larger, and millwork discreetly conceals essential storage. In all the projects we do, we take great care to accommodate the clients' needs and preferences. We always make sure to get to know our clients, listen to them, and take that knowledge as the first step in the redesign.

With that in mind, we reorganized the layout to create an apartment with two bedrooms and a den that can be converted into an additional guest bedroom. Originally, the dining room was completely cut off from the living room; we joined these two spaces to make the apartment, which isn't huge, feel more open and take better advantage of the light and views. Covering the ceiling in a silver tea paper added a note of glamour while reflecting light throughout.

One of the most exciting things about working with these clients is their discerning eye for art. Over the past few decades, they have amassed an exceptional collection, which was very much the impetus for the interior decor.

To allow for some freedom with the palette throughout the apartment—especially to complement the art—we used black and white as a connective thread. We began in the entry with a black-and-white stone floor in a beautiful waterjet pattern that I developed with Richard Goddard of Concept Studio. This graphic pattern bridges the classical and the modern and sets the tone for the rest of the apartment, where rich black floors and glossy doors offset punches of jewel tones, from the plush blue bedroom rug to the laser-cut teal dining room draperies to the low-slung matching sofa overlooking the bay—a favorite spot to sit on a rainy day. In the den, the walls and ceiling are lacquered in lapis, creating a radiant and inviting enclave and a perfect backdrop for the clients' Stanley Whitney painting. The effect is dazzling.

Given the relatively modest size of the apartment, the design had to be very efficient, and we tucked a lot of the utilitarian elements of the home away. There's a desk area and a laundry room hidden behind the kitchen; a portion of the molding in the entry conceals accoutrements for the dog; and one of the living room bookcases opens up to a secret wine room—that was Skurman and Smith's ingenious idea. It was so much fun to collaborate with them on these functional things, which are all but invisible but really make a home work for its residents. After all, design is all about the people and what they need. When you're able to do that with clients who have style and let you explore with them, magic happens.

PAGES 150-51: This chic, comfortable seating area in the living room features a tufted, crushed-velvet teal sofa and unique tables from Quintus. With its expansive views of the bay, it's an ideal spot for cocktails.

PAGE 152: In the entry, the barrel-vaulted ceiling and traditional millwork pay homage to the classical design of the building, while the waterjet pattern on the floor that we developed with Concept Studio hints at the modern kick to come.

PRECEDING PAGES: In the living room, tea paper on the ceiling lends a subtle glimmer, the addition of curved millwork and built-in shelves provides ample storage, and a mix of antique and contemporary furnishings speaks to the clients' urbane style. On the left, a pair of 1930s André Arbus Salon chairs with wood backs greets guests. Gabriel Scott's Harlow chandelier in smoked bronze and alabaster hovers above a 2007 painting by Louise Fishman.

OPPOSITE: A bold Stanley Whitney painting called for a strong backdrop, and the lapis-lacquered walls proved the perfect solution for this small-scale den that opens onto a terrace. The space can also be used as a guest room.

PRECEDING PAGES: Laser-cut-leather drapery panels conceal imperfect views without sacrificing sunlight, which has a warm, dappled effect in the dining room with its monumental Dakota Jackson dining table and suite of leather chairs. The valances and the silk backs of the chairs are hand-embroidered with art deco–style geometric motifs that I designed. A Jean De Merry chandelier glitters in front of a painting by Juan Uslé.

OPPOSITE: An arched alcove lends gravitas to the primary bedroom, which is sheathed in Belsize Tiles, a Fromental silk wallcovering that serves as a subdued backdrop for paintings by Julie Mehretu, over the custom bed, and Richard Diebenkorn, right. The antique art deco stools are covered in gauffrage velvet; the deep blue carpet is from Tai Ping.

ABOVE: In the small primary bath, *verre églomisé*–fronted cabinetry not only adds a shimmering patina but also makes the space appear larger; the soaring arch over the vanity contributes visual interest.

MODERNIST MASTER-PIECE

THE SUN ALSO RISES
ON MINIMALISM

LAS VEGAS / THE SUMMIT CLUB, NEVADA |

As interior designers, we are often called upon to work with architects and builders on ground-up projects such as this one. It was a particularly exciting commission because the owner, a longtime client, gave my partner, Derrick Davis, and me full creative rein to realize his vision for the home, from the site to the façade to every last interior detail.

A passionate modernist with a keen eye for collecting and a deep appreciation of clean lines, our client chose the Summit Club, located in the exclusive Las Vegas community of Summerlin and picturesquely situated between the Spring Mountains and Red Rock Canyon, for his new home, where he could host groups of friends, large and small. The vision for the house began with a stone-clad exterior that we thought would resonate with the surrounding desert landscape. At the time, a stone exterior was a standout in the community; it's now standard—a testament to the client's openness to creative risk-taking.

After advising on the exterior and on the selection of all the flooring materials, we turned our attention to the interiors. Given that the home's biggest asset was its magnificent view of both the city—all the way to the Strip—and the mountains through a wall of floor-to-ceiling windows in the main living area, our priority was to incorporate design elements that would keep all that glass from feeling cold. The cedar ceiling certainly helped, but we knew that the best way to warm up the modernist architecture was by incorporating unexpected textures, plush custom details, and rich materials. Shearling and bouclé upholstery, terrazzo floors, and a towering, raked-limestone chimneypiece scored by horizontal brass strips were subtle yet powerful touches that infuse the gathering space with a cozy ambiance.

This client has long been enamored with the Rat Pack—the renowned group of Las Vegas performers in the 1960s that included Frank Sinatra, Dean Martin, Sammy Davis Jr., and Joey Bishop—and he loves to entertain the way they did, in black-tie attire. The main living area in front of the fireplace is where the entertaining happens. The low-slung sectional sofa and other seating do not get in the way of the panoramic view. In the dining area on the opposite side of the space, a generous banquette has the inviting feel of a restaurant booth and provides additional seating.

A special feature of the house that we designed at the client's request is the pub, a chic, intimate space with a retro atmosphere, where guests feel like they've traveled back in time to imbibe and revel. Enveloped by lacquered, Hermès-orange walls and a bespoke wood ceiling treatment, this stylish lounge features a charming bar and a seating area anchored by leather-upholstered chairs and a long, plush, mohair-velvet sofa.

Knowing that a home office was also a must, we gave our client literally the best seat in the house, placing a desk that we designed in a mezzanine-like space above the living area with an expansive view of the Vegas skyline. To counterbalance the openness of the enormous space, we commissioned an artist to create a brutalist-inspired, three-dimensional collage in wood for the entire, two-story staircase wall. Installed piece by piece on-site, the collage may be the most unusual work of art in the client's collection, but it's just one of many pieces, which range from antique sculpture to specially commissioned paintings, including one fitted to cover the television over the fireplace.

Another showstopping wood treatment appears in the primary bedroom and adjoining sitting area, the walls of which are paneled in a stunningly striated Australian black walnut that is echoed on the backs of the Eames chairs. To soften all that hardwood, we designed a statement upholstered headboard that extends almost the entire length of the wall behind the bed and the custom, midcentury-inspired bedside tables. We opted for a neutral color palette in the primary bedroom suite to keep attention on the view of the hardscape and desert-friendly plantings of succulents outside and of the Spring Mountains beyond.

Sand, white, and natural wood tones are a winning color scheme for a minimalist interior, but the client's love of orange, fully embraced in the pub, is also incorporated in subtle ways throughout the house in the form of throw pillows and artwork. It appears in the guest bedroom, too, where my foster brother, decorative painter Robert O'Neil, created a graphic wall mural loosely inspired by the Sputnik style of the room's vintage light fixture. It's the perfect blend of retro, modern, and wholly original—like the house itself.

PAGES 162–63: In the entry, artist Peter Glassford created a site-specific wooden collage on the staircase wall.

PRECEDING PAGES: In the pub off the dining room, lacquered Hermès-orange walls, African mahogany screens, and a custom ceiling treatment create a chic backdrop for the mohair-velvet tuxedo sofa designed by Harte Davis and Billy Haines chairs. Next to the 1960s French floor lamp from Galerie Half, the antique slot machine is a cheeky nod to the Las Vegas setting.

OPPOSITE: In the double-height living area, the custom limestone chimneypiece, inset with horizontal brass strips, echoes the geometric architecture of the home and blends nicely with Woven's Allo rug in Sandstone. An artwork commissioned specially for the space slides up to reveal a television.

BELOW: Though the focus of the living area is on the sweeping view of the Spring Mountains and the Las Vegas Strip through the wall of windows, an eclectic mix enlivens the interior, including a Marmol Radziner–designed sofa, Ostuni stone Primitive coffee tables by Henge from MASS Beverly, a 1940s Fritz Hansen armchair upholstered in sheep hide from Denmark, a midcentury exotic-wood coffee table by Brazilian designer Percival Lafer, and a Robert Kuo coral-lacquered Pong bench.

OPPOSITE: A banquette built into a large, custom-designed mirrored cabinet gives the dining area the feel of a restaurant booth. The room's high ceilings allow ample space for the large-scale Thierry Jeannot light fixture, which illuminates a custom, oil-rubbed walnut dining table surrounded by Natasha Baradaran dining chairs.

RIGHT: In striking contrast to the airiness of the public spaces, the sitting area in the primary bedroom is clad in black Australian walnut, the variegated graining of which mimics that on the backs of the Eames lounge chairs and hand-carved walnut side table from Holly Hunt.

OVERLEAF: By covering the travertine floor with a silk rug and extending the headboard—upholstered in a Jack Lenor Larsen fabric—nearly the entire length of the wall behind the bed, we created a cocoon-like effect in the primary bedroom.

PRECEDING PAGES LEFT: Clean-lined custom cabinetry, slim Urban Electric Company sconces, and a sculptural column swivel chair keep the wife's bathroom simple yet elegant.

PRECEDING PAGES RIGHT: A frosted-glass dividing wall lets light into the bathroom while maintaining privacy.

RIGHT: In the guest bedroom, a custom mural by Robert O'Neil incorporates the client's beloved Hermès orange in a graphic motif that echoes the Sputnik-style chandelier. The custom nightstands are from Troscan, and the lamps are by Elan Atelier.

OVERLEAF: The outdoor spa is visible from the primary bedroom, so we decided to make it a focal point in front of the entrance façade. The house's exterior cuts a dramatic silhouette in the desert landscape.

HACIENDA STYLE

100 YEARS NEW AGAIN

PALM SPRINGS / OLD LAS PALMAS, CALIFORNIA |

Spanish-style houses have long been popular in the desert neighborhood of Old Las Palmas, and this century-old home—long called the Kellogg Estate because it was once owned by the heirs to the cereal-company fortune—is a perfect example of the type. But the home's promising exterior and architectural history hadn't protected it from bad renovations, including a disjointed layout that required bedrooms to be accessed from the outside, a mishmash of flooring and finishes, four different types of chimney, and a lot of other things that didn't make sense.

Our client was eager to give it a remodel befitting its architectural style. He was familiar with the Palm Springs area (his brother is another client of mine with homes in the desert) and loved both the location of the house and the idea of a Spanish-style home—he just wanted it to make sense. That meant taking the house down to the studs; the only element left intact was the roof. We found beautiful beams underneath layers of drywall, which was quite exciting and important as we reimagined the interior architecture and developed a new layout.

To me, designing the layout of a space is a combination of intuition and geometry. I love to study a room and try to figure out what feels appropriate, then think about the square footage needed to make that happen. In the case of this home, we did a lot of rearranging to open up and connect the spaces. Since the floor plan didn't account for a typical entryway, we created a sense of entry in the main living area with an overscale table and a bench flanked by recessed shelves. We organized the living area around the large-scale fireplace, which we clad in a custom, antique-inspired mantel. We also designed a series of arches to connect the living and private spaces, creating an enticing enfilade that brings architectural harmony. The clients have grown children who live on their own but visit frequently, so it was important for the spaces to flow one into the next but for everyone to have their own space when they want it.

Finishes—both interior and exterior—also helped to unify the space: we covered all the walls in warm, white plaster, refinished the stucco exterior, and used the floor treatments as a way to dictate the flow of the home while adding texture. Warm wood in the living and dining areas make way for terra-cotta tile, which runs from indoor rooms to the exterior. I worked with a local company to antique the tiles, which gives them a patina that suggests age commensurate with the original building.

One of my favorite details throughout the house is the decorative painting by artist Maria Trimbell. She and I have great synergy, and we love working together to develop ideas for interesting motifs. The designs she painted on the wide interior archways add pattern and texture while delineating their shape; the dado-like border she created in the primary bathroom has the effect of a mosaic pattern and ties together the tones in the checkerboard floor and the salvaged marble tub—the focal point of the room.

Texture comes, too, in the form of the eclectic mix of furniture throughout the home. Marrying elements like a sculptural, metal-framed rocking chair with a vintage wheeled cart (the one item retained from the original space!) that serves as a coffee table brings dynamism to the interior. As in many of my projects, this mix is complemented by an enticing roster of bold artwork.

The clients were adamant about introducing some color, and I thought pinks and oranges would nod to the home's Spanish roots without veering toward the garish. I tried to incorporate color in unexpected ways, whether in the form of the organic mulberry-bark paper in the sitting room or the beautifully veined red marble for the top of the kitchen island.

We carried this color story outside, where plush, reddish-orange armchairs surround an adobe-style fireplace. We worked with our frequent collaborator, the late landscape designer Marcello Villano, to revitalize the grounds, which was essential, given that nearly every room of the house opens to the exterior. The program we created features arcades and pathways connecting various zones, including the outdoor fireplace, the pool, and the canopied structure on the lawn in the rear that we reimagined as a Moorish-style lounge. For a home that once had neither rhyme nor reason, it's now an impressively cohesive and relaxing desert oasis.

PAGES 180–81: In lieu of a traditional entryway, an eighteenth-century Italian table from JF Chen, fronted by a bench and flanked by built-in shelving creates the effect of a grand entrance without losing the space to one. The stone dog is from Formations, the lamps are from Gregorius Pineo, and a Roman shade in a Porter Teleo fabric hints at the colors within.

PRECEDING PAGES: The home's rooms, once haphazardly and disjointedly laid out, are now connected by a series of archways that add architectural character and a sensible flow. Decorative painting by artist Maria Trimbell lends unexpected pattern and texture.

OPPOSITE: Connecting the formerly disjointed rooms created a series of peaceful, private outdoor spaces like this patio, where two Verano lounge chairs by Formations flank a Formations cast-stone side table. The artwork, by Paul Schick, is made of found branches.

PRECEDING PAGES: Behind a custom wrought-iron door manufactured in Los Angeles, the large living space presents an eclectic array of furniture, from collectible midcentury to found vintage pieces. The drapery fabric is by Porter Teleo, and the rug is from Hart's Rugs & Carpets.

OPPOSITE: The chandelier above the Formations dining table is an antique cross that Paul Ferrante transformed into a light fixture. Canterbury chairs from Formations are upholstered in a Jim Thompson stripe with raffia backing by Walfab.

OVERLEAF LEFT: An antique carpet, an armchair upholstered in a Schumacher print, and an organic mulberry-bark wallpaper introduce different shades of burnt orange into the sitting room, where a painting by Jason Kowalski nods to the homeowner's lifelong love of trains.

OVERLEAF RIGHT: The kitchen's textural backsplash is a custom tile from Concept Studio; the island's Old Church Red marble countertop ties into the red-orange palette throughout the interior.

RIGHT: In the primary bedroom, Kathy Jones's *Take Me with You* has pride of place. The custom bed is by Cache Furniture, the headboard is upholstered in a Romo fabric, and the hand-knotted Moroccan rug is from Woven. The Ron Dier table lamps are made from two book-matched pieces of tiger's eye.

OVERLEAF LEFT: Repainted in Farrow & Ball's Tanner's Brown, once-bland ceiling beams make an architectural statement over a custom bed in the guest room.

OVERLEAF RIGHT: Plans for a built-in soaking tub were scrapped when we came across this antique marble one, salvaged from an old house. It instantly became the centerpiece of the room.

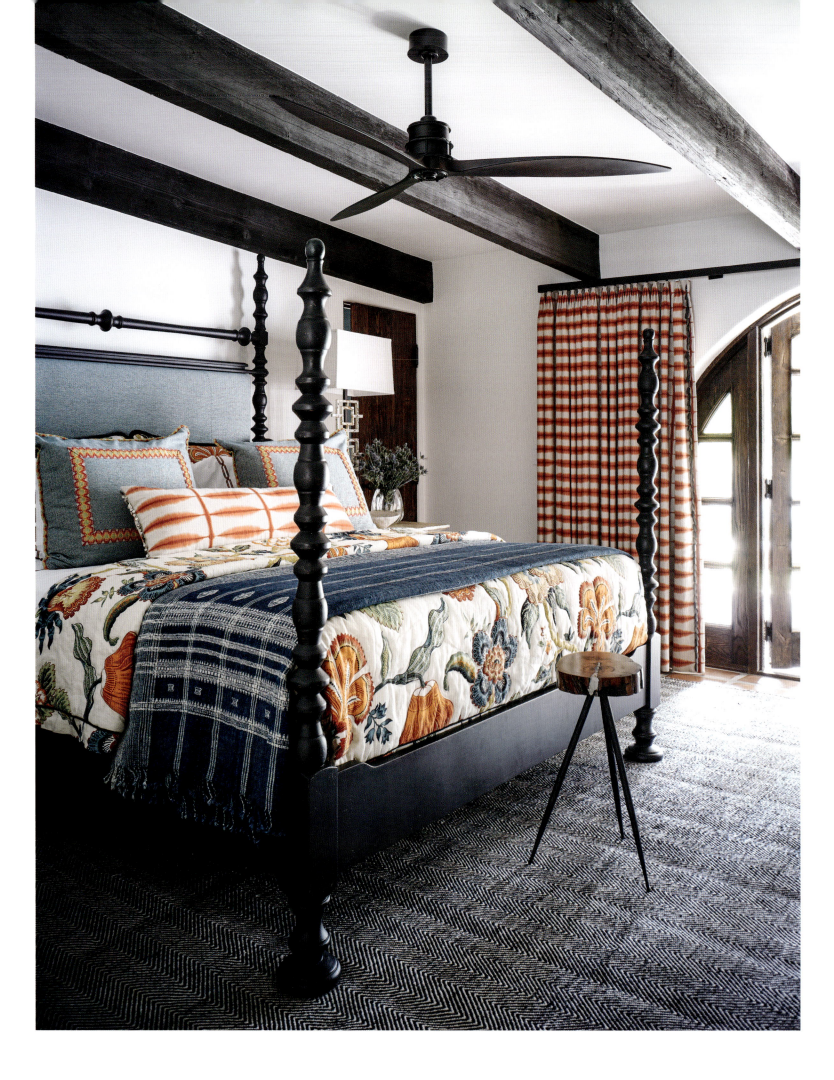

OPPOSITE: The freestanding outdoor fireplace, a beloved gathering spot, adds architectural interest to the exterior.

ABOVE: On the other side of the house, a Majorca daybed by Patio Productions, which we outfitted to resemble a Moorish-style lounge, invites relaxation.

NEWPORT CLASSIC RESTYLED

CHIC, CALIFORNIA, COMFORTABLE

There's a special kind of beauty to be found in contrast. That's certainly the case with this Newport Beach home, where classical proportions and furniture are juxtaposed with a collection of bold, contemporary art.

This is my second project for these clients, who had last remodeled their primary residence in the 1990s. Since then, their tastes and needs have evolved, and they were ready for a refresh. What hadn't changed, though, was their preference for classical, traditional style and contemporary art, so they tasked me with creating an updated spin on a classic home.

Thankfully, the existing layout still worked nicely for the clients, so we didn't need to rearrange the flow of the house. That allowed us to focus on the finishes, furnishings, and design details, which is always a treat. I began by fully reimagining the interior architecture, hand-drawing my concepts for every ceiling and doorway, as well as all the paneling and millwork. The walnut floors give warmth to the space and mimic the look of antique flooring, while marble in the entry hall and limestone in the garden room recall traditional architecture.

To elevate the architecture and provide a framework for the home's art and furniture, we added detailed molding and trim to every floor, ceiling, and cased opening. Our choice of millwork depended on the function of the room; for example, we opted for a pickled wood in the more casual family room and a high-gloss molding bordered by sophisticated light gray paint in the formal living room. In the garden room (also called the California Room), we installed soaring, steel-framed French doors and windows with elegantly arched motifs to complement the limestone floor and create the effect of a formal conservatory, an apt allusion for the wife, who loves to garden.

I love that each of the three living spaces provides a wholly unique experience within the house. The couple can gather around a fire set in a traditional marble fireplace in the living room, play backgammon at the Rose Tarlow game table under a massive, colorful

canvas in the family room, or enjoy views of the classically proportioned gardens from the California Room.

When I first met the couple in 2012, their taste veered toward classical art, but through our many conversations I brought them around to the idea of collecting modern art, and their collection has grown extensively since they first decorated this home. They're drawn to abstract and figurative work alike, giving us a broad range of works to incorporate into the design. My goal was to place art in unexpected ways. In the formal living room, with its neutral palette, traditional floral draperies, and antique desk, a trio of abstract canvases pack a graphic punch. In the family room, the textural nature of the pickled walls and subtle grid in the paneling are offset by Linda Christensen's rich, expressive painting. A trio of moody floral depictions bring an edge to the otherwise traditional primary bedroom.

The wife is an avid cook, and we created a bespoke design for the kitchen to suit her cooking style. All of the family's past kitchens had been dark in color, but here we went for a lighter, brighter look, with custom cream cabinetry, quartzite countertops, and a colorful window treatment, the floral pattern of which nods to the wife's penchant for gardens. We further brightened the space by adding a skylight over the chandelier, a trick we also employed in the primary bathroom, where we added a laylight, bringing additional natural light into the relatively small space.

Both the husband and the wife were drawn to a blue-and-beige color scheme, which, in the wrong hands, can feel dated. In keeping with our vision of an updated classic, we played on this pairing throughout the house in ways that give each room a unique feel while retaining it as a connective thread throughout. In the family room, for example, a striking turquoise marble fireplace surround is an unexpected focal point against the warm wood walls—and a contemporary foil to the antique carpet. Draperies and pillows with different blue prints in each room pop against the neutral upholstery, and even the rugs we sourced have blue in their patterns. It was such a pleasure to reinvigorate an interior and give our clients' home a new look: cool but comfortable, classic yet fresh, artful and understated.

PAGES 198–99: Soaring, steel-rimmed French doors give the garden room the feel of a conservatory and provide ample views of the landscape. Outdoor furniture from Formations and draperies by Perennials mix with a Dennis & Leen lantern and a custom table.

PAGE 200: We gave the clients' own buffet new life by refinishing it and setting it in a hall beneath an antique mirror inset into the millwork. Classical moldings frame the view into the kitchen.

PRECEDING PAGES: Deft pairing of traditional elements—an antique Persian rug, embroidered Cowtan & Tout draperies, Rose Tarlow side tables—with bold abstract art on walls painted a stony, gray-green Farrow & Ball hue has a vibrant effect in the formal living room.

OPPOSITE: The dining room presents another spin on the couple's preferred blue-and-beige palette, with Queen Anne armchairs from Dennis & Leen, upholstered in a Templeton fabric, around a walnut dining table by Gregorius Pineo. The glass-fronted cabinet, once a dark ebony, was refinished in ivory for a brighter take.

OPPOSITE: A monumental oil canvas by Linda Christensen overlooks a Rose Tarlow game table in the more casual family room, which is paneled in a pickled oak. The dining chairs are antique and painted with a faux-bone finish.

BELOW: A turquoise marble fireplace surround is both an unexpected take on the home's blue-and-beige color scheme and an energetic foil to the pickled-oak millwork. The furniture is an elegant yet comfortable mix, including a Rose Tarlow sofa, a custom open-back settee, Hancock & Moore armchairs, and a coffee table from Gregorius Pineo, set atop an antique Persian rug from Woven.

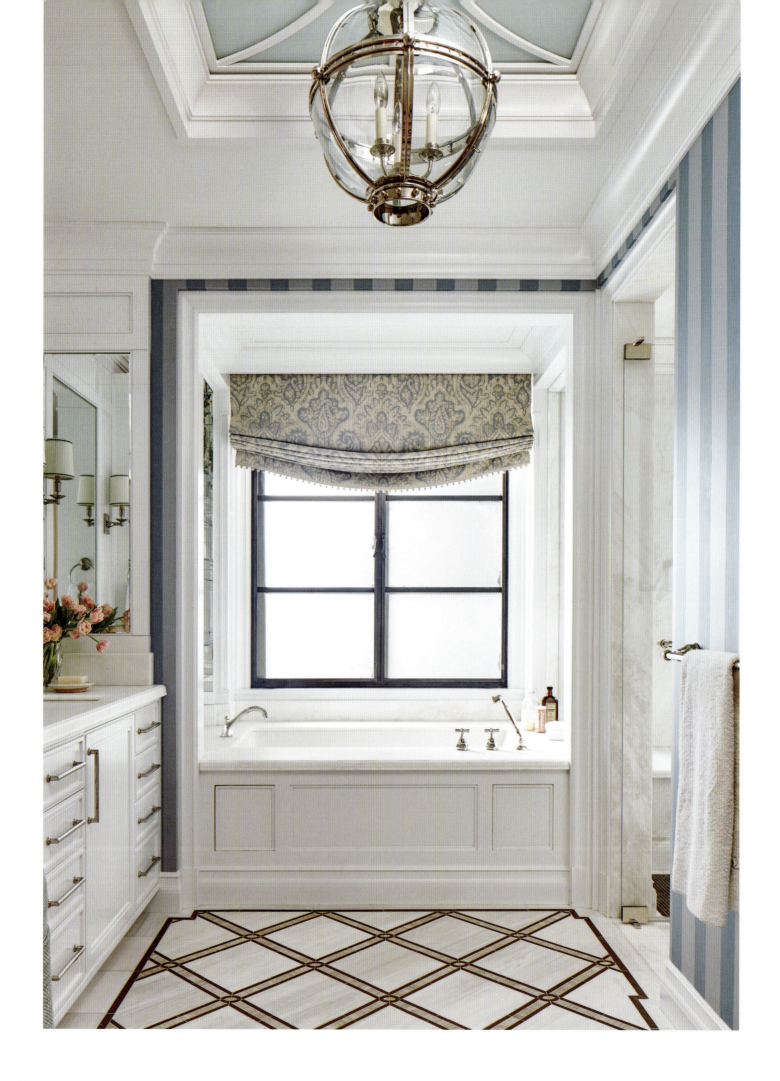

OPPOSITE: The primary bath presents a slightly brighter take on the couple's preferred blue-and-beige palette. Building the tub into an alcove beneath the sole window maximizes the small space, and installing a laylight above the chandelier brings in additional natural light.

BELOW: The primary bedroom's walls are lined in a fawn-colored silk upholstery, selected to coordinate with the room's antique carpet. A bed by Rose Tarlow is flanked by a pair of parchment nightstands for another softly textural touch.

FRENCH FANTASY

LA VIE EN ROSE
IN NEWPORT COAST

NEWPORT COAST / PELICAN HILL, CALIFORNIA |

So much of my work is about curating a balanced mix of old and new—the tried and the true—that it can be invigorating to undertake a project where the client wants a very specific style. That was the case with this home for a stylish Francophile and her husband who wanted to incorporate eighteenth-century France into a home in Newport Coast, bringing a Continental ambiance to a California setting in a way that felt authentic but adapted to modern life.

The clients are connoisseurs of European antiques, so we began from a place of deep knowledge, but wherever we didn't have the requisite background, we dove into research. This entailed spending many hours poring over books about the châteaux of the Loire Valley, studying period drawings of French architecture, and dissecting eighteenth-century floor plans.

Of course, even a home as artfully considered as this one has to be livable, so there were certain concessions to be made—mostly in terms of scale. With antiques, especially chairs, size can be an issue; people were smaller in the eighteenth century. The husband is six foot five, so, quite simply, we needed seating that would accommodate him. The challenge became to find—or, more often, custom-make—furniture with the proportions and details of European antiques, but adapted slightly in size, so that it both looks authentic and is comfortable for the client.

When we did have to make concessions for modern sizing, it became all the more important to imbue these elements with the kind of detail that would befit their antique ancestors. In the case of the dining chairs, for example, which we sourced in a larger size than comparable antiques, we created a crest based on eighteenth-century examples and had it embroidered on the chair backs, inventing a bit of faux history for the home.

This kind of designer trickery is perhaps most evident in the kitchen, where eighteenth- and twenty-first-century demands are obviously vastly different. We hid appliances and warming drawers behind paneling and tucked blenders and coffee machines into custom cabinetry.

One of the stars of this home is the dramatic, intricate millwork and plasterwork, all of which we designed and hand-sketched based on period examples, including the strapwork on the first-floor ceilings; the medallion surrounding the chandelier in the entrance hall, inset in a gilded dome; the elaborate cornices throughout the home; and the millwork framing the panels of de Gournay silk wallcovering in the dining room.

We're lucky to have many craftspeople in California who are knowledgeable about historical detailing and skilled at working in those styles. JP Weaver Company executed the millwork and moldings, and they were fastidious about faithfully replicating historical examples. Each detail required a sample, and sometimes it took eight or ten samples to get it right, but the result is well worth that level of meticulousness.

I worked closely with my incredible drapery workroom on the window treatments through-out the home, all of which are also based on historical examples and rendered in traditional silk damask. I researched eighteenth-century French draperies and sketched my favorites; my drapery maker then scaled them proportionately and made mockups. It was quite fun to take on the challenge of creating something new within the parameters of a period style.

I searched for the better part of a year for the perfect rug for the primary bedroom, which is swathed in a luminescent, hand-painted silver de Gournay leaf paper embellished with silk embroidery. When it became clear that a rug in the correct size didn't exist, we found an antique one and had it re-created, scaling it up to fit the space. The true test of these reproductions came in placing them alongside the clients' collection of real antiques, and I'm happy to say that, in many instances, it's difficult to tell which is which.

As we were working on the house, the client was becoming more and more well-versed in French art. By the time we were ready to install, she had amassed a robust collection of authentic eighteenth- and nineteenth-century French paintings. A William-Adolphe Bouguereau portrait hangs over the dramatic black marble fireplace in the library; the primary bedroom's luminous silver walls are the backdrop to canvases by Luigi Loir and Léon Lhermitte; a trio of eighteenth-century botanicals hold pride of place between the guest room's twin canopy beds. That final layer, a testament to the client's continued curiosity and deep passion for design, is the home's true pièce de résistance.

PAGES 210–11: The spectacular antique Aubusson rug was the jumping-off point for the main living room, where silk draperies trimmed with a Samuel & Sons fringe flank soaring windows over a thoughtful assortment of eighteenth-century furniture.

PRECEDING PAGES: The double-height entrance with its curved double stair is a showcase for exquisite millwork by JP Weaver Company, wrought-iron balustrades, and an antique chandelier, the light of which is reflected in the gilded dome above.

OPPOSITE: The formal living room is a showcase for the clients' spectacular collection of European antiques, framed in the double-height space with custom touches like elongated windowpanes, overscale door casings, and elegant strapwork adorning the ceiling.

PRECEDING PAGES: Green silk scenic panels by de Gournay are set into intricate millwork in the dining room, where the backs of Louis XVI dining chairs from C. Mariani Antiques feature a crest designed to resemble eighteenth-century examples.

RIGHT: In the kitchen, paneled cabinetry, designed in collaboration with Donna Pozdro, and marble countertops conceal modern amenities such as coffeemakers and appliances. We designed the lanterns with Paul Ferrante.

OVERLEAF: A William-Adolphe Bouguereau portrait hangs above a black marble mantel in the library, the more intimate scale of which makes it a favorite destination for after-dinner drinks. The two marble-topped chests and gilt mirrors are eighteenth century, the antique rug is from Mansour, the sofa and armchairs are by Rose Tarlow, and the antique pillows are from Y & B Bolour.

PRECEDING PAGES: The primary bedroom's elaborate plaster frieze and ceiling ornamentation, custom drapery, and matching *lit à couronne* were the result of extensive research into period examples. Eighteenth-century English giltwood side chairs and a pair of Louis XVI gilded chests resonate with the metallic thread in the embroidered de Gournay wallcovering, which is complemented by the Cowtan & Tout silk draperies.

RIGHT: In the seating area of the primary bedroom, paintings by Luigi Loir (over the mantel) and Léon Lhermitte are bathed in natural light from the adjacent loggia. The rug is a replica of a French antique, scaled up to fit the space.

OPPOSITE: With a freestanding English tub, sumptuous Colefax and Fowler drapery, and paneling that hides all the necessities of a modern bathroom, the wife's daily bath becomes a luxurious routine under the glow of an antique Baccarat chandelier.

BELOW: A pair of twin beds in one guest room accommodates visiting nieces and nephews. The walls are covered in Lille, an archival fabric from Rose Cumming.

RIGHT: With its custom, hand-knotted, Central Asian–style rug, hand-tooled-leather walls, and reclining armchairs in sumptuous mohair upholstery, the screening room invites relaxation.

OVERLEAF: The home's landscaping follows the same inspiration as the interiors, with boxwood hedges, brick pathways, and a central fountain forming a scaled-down take on a formal French garden.

A HOUSE
FOR ALL
SEASONS

PRECEDING PAGES: With its antique Flemish tapestry, contemporary sculpture, and classic skirted table, the entryway sets the tone for the home's careful balance of old and new decorative accessories.

RIGHT: In the living room, neutral textural elements like the overscale stone coffee table, the Tai Ping rug, and sofas and arm-chairs upholstered in an ivory quilted fabric from Schumacher are punctuated with exuberant, multicolored textiles, including the slipper chairs, clad in Clarence House's Budapest, and custom-made pillows, which offset the clean linearity of the home's refined architecture.

ECLECTIC, ELEGANT ...
AND THEY'RE GREAT COOKS

When two adults, each with their own home, collections, and style, get together with all the best intentions of becoming Mr. and Mrs., there is always the challenge of combining "yours" and "mine" into "ours." This was the case with desert-loving clients who had been living in the Palm Springs area for years (she in Indian Wells, he in Rancho Mirage), first individually, then together while dating. When they got married, they decided it was high time to create a home that reflected the two of them and their happy life together. The question was, where?

The husband, who is from Canada, lived on the edge of a Jack Nicklaus–designed golf course in scenic Rancho Mirage. With an exceptional location and promising floor plan, his house became the chosen one, even though it was dark and claustrophobic. The couple called on us to give it a fresh new design and make it a place they could call home: collected, joyful, and full of friends.

Working in tandem with architect Thomas Jakway and general contractor Damian Trevor, we endeavored to retain the best features of the existing home—easy, livable layout; one-story floor plan; plenty of outdoor access—while stripping away earlier design decisions. We specified bold and textural finishes: plastered walls, chiseled Israeli limestone floors, metal-framed windows, polished nickel–framed cabinetry, and thick butcher block. The overall intent was to clean and open up the space, making it feel up-to-date while also creating a chic backdrop for an eclectic collection of art and furnishings.

One thing that makes this home so dynamic is the clients' unusually diverse mix of art and antiques, ranging from the seventeenth century to the twenty-first. Accordingly, our vision for the design of the interior was to give a nod to the traditional, but update it with unexpected textures, shapes, and materials. The wife was eager to incorporate her truly eclectic collection of antiques and contemporary items from her previous home into the new house. For us, it was a fun challenge to find new ways to showcase them.

Nowhere is that vision more on display than in the entryway, where we set the tone for the interior by pairing a seventeenth-century Flemish tapestry from the wife's previous home with a clean-lined, glass-topped table skirted with a fabric in an Ottoman-inspired pattern and two velvet X-stools. An animal-skin rug and a dog sculpture lend an interesting, unexpected touch. In the dining room, a set of elegant, saber-leg chairs from Dennis & Leen around an antique mahogany table is mixed with a pair of skirted Gregorius Pineo chairs. The table's rich color is offset by the cerulean upholstery uniting both styles of seating. Both the husband and wife had collected traditional paintings before they met but have since become interested in more contemporary works, so we rounded out their collection with more recent pieces that engage in a lively dialogue with their eighteenth- and nineteenth-century art.

One aspect that this couple was very specific about was the palette. Her preference was to have a neutral scheme with a few pops of color, whereas his was to include some yellow. If yellow is his favorite color, hers is a bluish green, so incorporating both became a symbolic way to represent their domestic merger—and provide energetic accents against the mostly neutral backdrop.

The couple are big entertainers—and fabulous cooks—so hosting amenities were also top of mind when we were designing the public areas of the home. In the kitchen, we curved one end of the island to accommodate a round table, so that when friends are over, they can sit and chat with the couple without being in the way of the cooking. We echoed the curvature of the island in the adjacent wet bar, which features all sorts of hidden and open storage for serving ware. The entertaining accoutrements extend to the exterior, too, where we worked with the late Marcello Villano, our frequent collaborator in the desert, on the landscape. In keeping with the changes to the architecture, we pared back many of the exterior elements, resulting in a more clean-lined landscape dotted with native and drought-resistant plants that frame the views of the golf course and mountains without competing with them. We incorporated a fire pit, smoker, pizza oven, and Argentinean grill into several areas of hardscape, fully equipping the couple for any sort of outdoor hosting, dining, and entertaining. And we provided a variety of seating options, from dining and sitting areas to chaises longues around the pool. Because when the view is this good, you may just want to stay outside.

PRECEDING PAGES: The clients' antique table and sideboard get a jolt of new energy from the electric-blue upholstery on the Dennis & Leen chairs and from the Brunschwig & Fils Lightning Bolt upholstery on the side chairs. The artwork is a compelling mix from the clients' collection.

OPPOSITE: The husband's love of yellow sets the tone in the TV room, where a custom sectional sofa, a trio of selenite-topped tables, and draperies in a nubby Ralph Lauren fabric with a Schumacher ikat border radiate a sunny warmth against the textural wallcovering from Newcastle Fabrics. An armchair and a throw pillow covered in a Kravet flamestitch-patterned velvet pull out the colors in the painting above.

BELOW: Clean, white cabinetry trimmed in polished nickel and quartzite counter-tops give the kitchen a fresh look, but it is, above all, highly functional for clients who are avid cooks. The two islands (one topped by quartzite, the other by butcher block) allow for parallel meal prep, and translucent cabinet fronts make tableware easily accessible.

OPPOSITE: Nestling a custom kitchen table by Keith Fritz into the curved end of one island provides a place for friends to gather while the couple cook. The chairs, upholstered in a Lee Jofa fabric on the outsides and Perennial's Sunshine fabric on the seats and backs, bring welcome color to the space. The adjacent bar area provides ample storage for entertaining accoutrements.

OPPOSITE: The wife's color preference is accommodated in her bathroom, where a freestanding Crosswater tub is surrounded by walls swathed in a blue Schumacher chinoiserie pattern printed on grasscloth. Neutral tile floors from Concept Studio echo the limestone throughout the house.

BELOW: The use of a bright ikat by Lee Jofa to upholster the headboard and for the window treatment makes the guest room bright, friendly, and welcoming—ideal for clients who love to host.

BEAUTY AND THE BEACH

POLISHED AND ROUGH,
DARK AND LIGHT BY THE SEA

When you work with a client for more than two decades on several houses, you have the luxury of creating site-specific designs for different aspects of their life. This home rounds out a perfect trifecta of city, mountain, and beach living for this client and her family.

The client had lived in Newport Beach, California, a long time ago and has always loved the area. She fell in love with this architecturally singular house in nearby China Cove for its location right on the beach. Unsurprisingly, her children love it as well.

The house, originally built by architect Ade Collie in 2007, is unique in the area for its Balinese-influenced architecture. It is a study in contrasts, made of rough-hewn stone combined with polished mahogany. The clients loved all the texture and the meandering, indoor-outdoor layout. They enlisted me to reimagine it for their life by retaining all the texture, accenting the interiors with elements of black and white and polished metals to offset the stone walls, and envisioning creative ways to incorporate their ever-growing collection of art. I loved the chiseled feel of the stone walls; their heft and texture became the jumping-off point for the project.

We set the tone right in the entry, where a mirror by Nicole Hollis for McGuire with a shaggy raffia trim hangs above a sculptural, live-edge table that looks like a huge chunk of weathered wood that had washed ashore. With the ocean as our inspiration, we cast about for an existing piece of art for the stairwell of the winding staircase just off the entry but realized that a commissioned piece would serve the space best. We wanted something original that felt beachy and brought in some new texture. As the wall was curved, traditional framed art was out of the question, so we enlisted Jim Olarte, an artist from Laguna Beach, to create a suspended rope sculpture. The textural, three-dimensional work draws the eye to the stairwell and casts enchanting shadows on the wall behind it.

As in so many of my projects, the art played an integral role in the interiors. We worked with the client to seek out specific places for pieces in her collection. The mesmerizing effect of a Damien Hirst butterfly mandala is perfect above the living room fireplace; a word painting by Mel Bochner brings color and levity to the dining room. This client truly buys what she loves, so the collection is extremely varied—from George Condo to Auguste Renoir—which made it especially fun to create conversations among the pieces throughout the home.

As impressive as the blue-chip art and intriguing architecture are, the home is far from a museum. It is deeply, comfortably livable, as the living room illustrates. The space is expansive, with one end opening out to the oceanfront patio and the other facing the indoor courtyard and the kitchen and casual dining area beyond. To maximize the usefulness and comfort of the room, we split the square footage into two, with one seating area around the fireplace and another by the ocean-facing windows. A game table in a corner is such a hit that the family often eats dinner there.

One of the magical aspects of the house is the openness of the layout, which makes the most of its oceanfront location. The home is truly designed for indoor-outdoor living; the doors are always open to let the sea breeze waft in. It's equally comfortable to sit on the oceanfront terrace or in the home's courtyard garden, originally envisioned by Terry Hart, a contributing landscape designer at the Getty Museum. The courtyard, which is in the heart of the home and accessed from the kitchen and dining areas, not only provides a private outdoor living space but also drenches the interiors in natural light.

With so much of the house feeling open, light, and interconnected, the more enclosed spaces take on a special allure. For the office and bathrooms, we leaned into the richness of polished mahogany, which brings an elegance and luminosity to the ceilings. Though the clients loved the Balinese-influenced architecture, we didn't want it to feel like a pastiche, so it was important to marry those traditional elements with more modern and unexpected ones such as a black-tiled bathtub, a graphic wallpaper, and elegant pieces of furniture. In the powder room, we paired a tropical leaf–patterned Phillip Jeffries wallpaper with a backlit onyx sink. In the guest room, an artful black-and-white botanical wallcovering from Schumacher offers a lighter take on tropical. Here, it's all about the balance between the polished and the rough—and creating a refined but comfortable living environment by the sea.

PAGES 244–45: A fringed mirror by Nicole Hollis for McGuire, a live-edge console, and a woven Phillip Jeffries wallpaper set a textural tone in the entryway of the beachfront home.

PAGES 246–47: The main living space is divided into multiple areas to facilitate large and small gatherings alike. A shag rug from Woven provides a comfortable base for an assortment of modern, sculptural furniture, the low-slung silhouettes and neutral palette of which don't detract from the ocean views.

PRECEDING PAGES: A graphic Damien Hirst butterfly mandala, one of many museum-quality pieces throughout the home, pops against the rough-hewn stone wall. The armchair and ottoman are by A. Rudin.

OPPOSITE: The round mirror, round macassar ebony dining table, and custom curved banquette contribute to a circle theme in the dining room, where a Mel Bochner canvas adds a jolt of cheeky color.

PRECEDING PAGES: The home's central courtyard is visible from the living room, where an A. Rudin sectional provides ample, comfortable seating. The Ferrante coffee table includes a built-in footrest for additional comfort.

OPPOSITE: In the powder room, a backlit onyx sink illuminates a subtly tropical Phillip Jeffries wallpaper.

BELOW: The central courtyard provides a private alfresco living space. It is outfitted with Kannoa seating upholstered in a Perennials fabric and stools from Made Goods.

OVERLEAF LEFT: The curved stairwell provided the perfect backdrop for a custom artwork by Laguna Beach–based Jim Olarte, whose rope sculpture casts intriguing shadows on the wall behind.

OVERLEAF RIGHT: A Damien Hirst painting has pride of place at the top of the stairs.

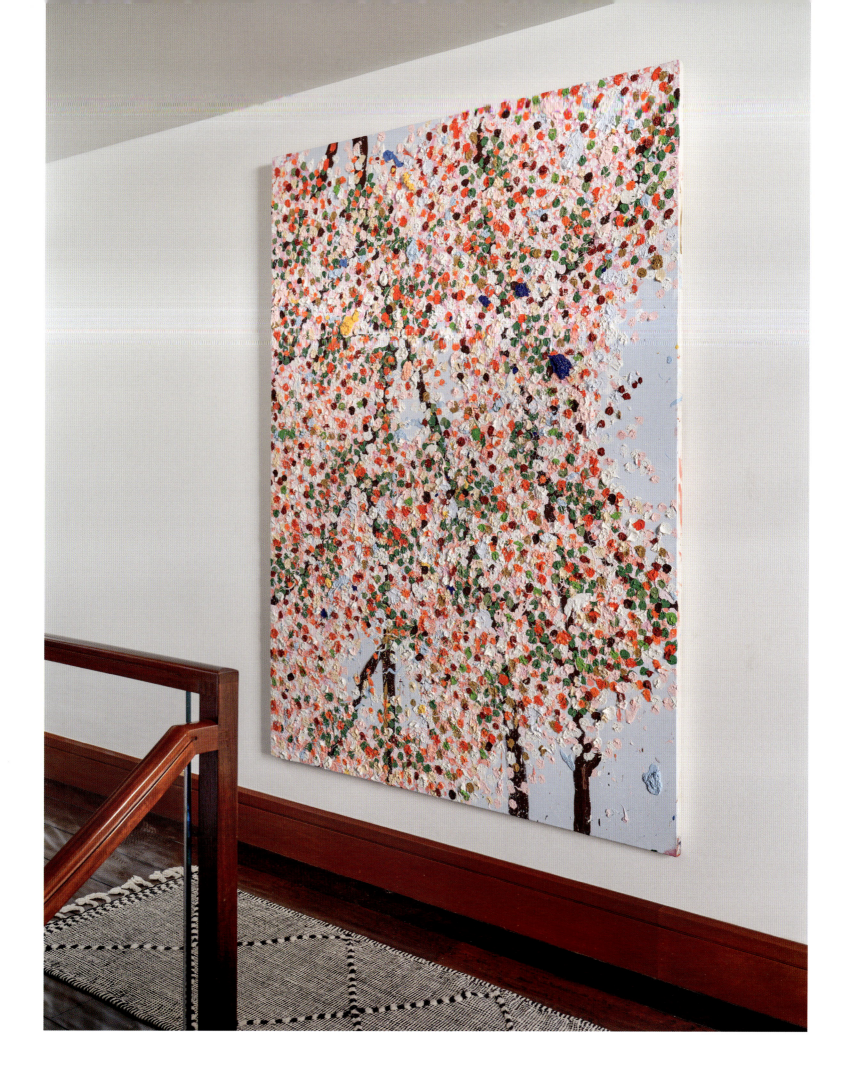

OPPOSITE: A straw wallcovering from Phillip Jeffries offsets the sleek mahogany paneling on the ceiling of the primary bedroom, where a Hodsoll McKenzie fabric packs a graphic punch on the bed and a Marc Chagall painting adorns the entry to the room.

ABOVE: A black-and-white Schumacher wallpaper offers a minimalist take on a tropical motif in a guest room. The custom nightstand features a raffia drawer and a mahogany top on a steel base; the lamp is from Visual Comfort.

DESERT VOGUE

CONTEMPORARY CANVAS FOR A BLUE-CHIP ART COLLECTION

INDIAN WELLS / THE RESERVE CLUB, CALIFORNIA |

With its rugged desert landscape and bighorn sheep wandering amid the native plants, the Reserve Club, in Indian Wells, California, is a far cry from the pristine palms and manicured lawns of neighborhoods in the nearby resort towns around Palm Springs. It's also not necessarily where you'd expect to find a museum-worthy art collection. But for my longtime clients—passionate art collectors who grew up in Arizona and found the terrain familiar—it proved the perfect backdrop for an idyllic, artful desert home.

This was the second house I did for these clients, and we had developed a strong design language to address their preferences, which has made working together a fluid, creatively energizing process. We collaborated with architect Stewart Woodard to conceive this desert getaway from the ground up. The vision was an architecturally modern house, but one that exuded warmth—after that, they really let us run with it.

The exterior was designed with the aim of incorporating the house into its landscape and setting the tone for the kind of modern, cosmopolitan desert living you find inside. We balanced the more angular lines of the house with curved, battered exterior walls and created texture with a mix of materials and a carefully considered sculpture program set among the plantings.

Inside, almost every room has access to the exterior, with wide casings and expansive sliding doors meant to encourage the kind of indoor-outdoor lifestyle that attracts so many people to the desert. We made use of both interior and exterior skylights to impart an open, airy feel to windowless spaces like the kitchen and the lower level. The architecture also exists in service to the clients' incredible art, a thoughtful, wide-reaching collection amassed over the better part of two decades. The work ranges from glass pieces by the likes of Dale Chihuly and William Morris to sculpture, painting, and even video art acquired when it was a fledgling medium. Some works, like Joan Brown's *Sarah Vaughan at the Sands*, are fittingly Palm Springs specific, while others, including Wayne Thiebaud's *Deli Bowls*, are career highlights of international recognition.

Working with a collection of such significance offers a special opportunity for dialogue between art and interiors. To connect the main and lower levels, for example, we designed a cantilevered spiral staircase, lit with fiber optics to illuminate the substantial John Chamberlain sculpture that sits at its base. To display the couple's glass collection while maintaining the open-plan layout, we created a freestanding fireplace surround fitted with titanium panels and inset shelves. These are but two instances of our artful approach to custom details; others include the waterjet tile patterns on the kitchen backsplash and entry floor and the seamless, made-to-order carpets.

As for the decoration, we took our cues from the wife's fashion sensibility. She wears black, brown, gray, navy, and sometimes a pop of red—and that's the color scheme she wanted for the house. Such a clearly defined palette allowed us to focus our attention on the optimal placement of the art; it also encouraged us to lean into texture and materiality, which bring a certain depth to the interiors.

The monumental stone table in the entry—a Catalonian antique—was the first piece of furniture purchased for the home, and it sets an apt tone. It may resemble a typical entry table in shape and scale, but, with its highly textured surface and substantial weight, it's both rugged and modern—much like the property as a whole.

We prioritized unexpected applications and combinations—such as wood and stainless-steel cabinetry—and uncommon materials like black walnut, steel tile, and mulberry-bark wallcoverings throughout the home's public and private spaces, which include two casitas. These clients have a deep appreciation for the details of a project, which, as Charles Eames famously said, "make the design," so no square inch escaped attention. Every stretch of molding, custom switch plate, inset outlet, handle, pull, and hanging wire was carefully hand-drawn before being translated by our trusted fabricators and installers. That, you might say, makes the home a work of art in itself.

It's been fifteen years since we completed this house, and while dozens of guests have come and gone, children and grandchildren have grown up, and the art collection has continued to expand, nearly every element of the architecture and design has remained just as it was when we first installed it. Good design, as they say, is timeless.

PAGES 260–61: A monumental sixteenth-century stone table in the entryway is in rugged contrast to the polished, toffee-colored, honed-limestone floor from Concept Studio. The large canvas by Joan Brown and the Deborah Butterfield horse sculpture hint at the substantial art collection inside.

PRECEDING PAGES: A custom spiral staircase with translucent treads lit with fiber optics illuminates an iridescent John Chamberlain sculpture at its base on the lower level, which houses a screening room, billiards table, and video-game nook. The painting is by Linda Christensen.

OPPOSITE: In the living room, an art deco armchair upholstered in a traditional woven floral fabric by Glant is unexpectedly paired with an oversize abstract work by Christian Rosa purchased in Portugal.

RIGHT: Architect Stewart Woodard designed a pavilion-like house with a canopy roof that allows light in but protects the interiors from harsh sunlight. In the living room, a custom, freestanding shelving system around the fireplace serves as both a television cabinet and display case for the clients' collection of glass and ceramic art.

BELOW: Wenge wood panels inset into stainless-steel frames give the kitchen a streamlined, retro look. The counters are a combination of stainless steel and polished soapstone.

OPPOSITE: In the dining room, a blown-glass work by Dale Chihuly echoes the colors in the Sam Francis painting. The chandelier over the oval Therien dining table was designed by Robert Kuo for Baker.

OPPOSITE: An abstract diptych is a perfect backdrop for a pair of art deco armchairs and a table from the noted twentieth-century San Francisco dealer Ed Hardy. The geometric-patterned wool-and-silk carpet is from Hart's Rugs & Carpets.

BELOW: The main wall in the primary bedroom is lined in macassar ebony. Richard Diebenkorn's *Untitled #1* from his *Clubs and Spades* series hangs over the Argos bed, made of zebrawood.

RIGHT: In the primary bath, his-and-her vanities and a soaking tub are clad in macassar ebony with an unusually prominent grain. Its variegated coloring is complemented by the custom Maya Romanoff wallpaper. The painting is by Joan Brown.

OVERLEAF: The game room on the lower level boasts a steel billiards table from David Sutherland and a custom foosball table beneath a unique ceiling of uplit suspended beams. The custom Ron Dier sconces, Michael Berman sofas, McGuire barstools, and Stark carpet ensure hours of leisure fun.

PAGES 276-77: The clients' art collection continues outside, where a ceramic sculpture by Jun Kaneko is the focal point at the end of a reflecting pool. Designed by Greg Grisamore, the landscaping features a wall of craggy rocks and desert plants, reflecting the Reserve Club's natural surroundings.

WITH LOVE AND GRATITUDE, I DEDICATE THIS BOOK TO MY HUSBAND, JOHN COMBS, WHOSE STEADFAST VISION, UNBRIDLED SUPPORT, AND ENDLESS ENCOURAGEMENT INSPIRE ME TO PURSUE EXCELLENCE IN ALL THAT I DO.

I would not be where I am today without the love and guidance of my parents, Mel and Charlotte Harte. I adored my mother for her style, fashion panache, and impeccable taste. She left us too soon—but she left me with great memories of going antiquing with her. My stepmother, Dorothy Harte, gave me the wings to fly, broadening my world beyond the San Fernando Valley, where I grew up.

As I reflect on forty extraordinary years in interior design, I am filled with immense gratitude for the journey that has brought me here—and for the trust and vision of my clients, many of whom have returned time and again, allowing me the privilege of transforming their homes into spaces of beauty, elegance, and comfort. Your confidence in my work has been the foundation of my success, and for that I am profoundly thankful.

This monumental body of work could only be possible with the support of some very special associates.

To my brilliant business partner, Derrick Davis—who joined me in 2016 and quickly became indispensable—heartfelt appreciation for being my wingman in bringing the homes featured in this book to life. I am especially excited as we embark on this new chapter as Harte Davis Interior Design.

A special thank-you to my "design sister," Donna Pozdro, an incredible partner in developing the interior architectural details in my projects for more than twenty-five years.

I am profoundly grateful for my brother in both life and art, Robert O'Neil, whose creative sensibilities, wall murals, and artistic touches have enriched so many of our projects.

Great appreciation to senior designer Megan Pulfer—your talent and commitment have been instrumental in shaping the essence of our work. And to our longtime collaborator Joyce Legate for your passion and perseverance.

Richard Goddard, thank you for being my stone soulmate, and kudos to your terrific team—Michelle Venegas, Lindsay Manning, and Melissa Roth—for sourcing the perfect stone, tile, and surface materials for our projects.

I am truly grateful to my publicist, Tamar Mashigian, whose insight and belief in my work have propelled it into the public eye over the past two decades. Your dedication to bringing this book to life has been invaluable.

To the extraordinarily talented photographer Douglas Friedman and stylist Anita Sarsidi, my gratitude for the superb images and for encouraging us to aim high and seek out a publisher worthy of our work. And to Trevor Tondro, John Merkl, and Björn Wallander, I so appreciate how beautifully you've photographed our projects.

Thank-yous all around to Vendome's Mark Magowan, Beatrice Vincenzini, and Jacqueline Decter, to book agent Cynthia Conigliaro for bringing my first monograph to publication, and to Rita Sowins for her beautiful, artistic design.

To the architects, builders, landscape designers, and incredible project partners with whom I've moved mountains—both literally and figuratively—I am thankful.

I am grateful to my dear friend Lee Stanton McCamon, whose vast knowledge of architecture and antiques and our many conversations and journeys have provided insights into timeless design, and to my close friend Nathan Ure for encouraging me to take this leap.

To Robert Rufino, whose keen editorial vision continues to inspire me; to Israel Serna, for scouting projects for publication; and to Harry Boskase, for your attuned eye in all things aesthetic—thank you.

Kudos to Jennifer Ellsworth, the quiet force behind the curtain, for ensuring that every moving part works in perfect harmony up front.

And last but not least, a round of applause for the talented artisans and vendors whose exquisite furnishings, fabrics, and decorative arts grace these pages, particularly Alex Menegaz of Paul Ferrante Inc. (creative savant in all things custom lighting, furniture, and objets d'art), Mike Cohen (creative custom furniture craftsman), Art Pena and Duane Longworth (upholstery visionaries), Wilfredo and Will Flores (our finish gurus), and Mark and Claudia Seay (sublime window coverings).

Here's to four decades of design excellence. I wish every project could be featured on these pages—but there are many more to come.

SHELDON HARTE

ACKNOWLEDGMENTS

The Refined Home: Sheldon Harte
First published in 2025 by The Vendome Press
Vendome is a registered trademark of The Vendome Press LLC

VENDOME PRESS US
PO Box 566
Palm Beach, FL 33480

VENDOME PRESS UK
Worlds End Studio
132–134 Lots Road
London SW10 0RJ

www.vendomepress.com

ISBN: 978-0-86565-473-0

PUBLISHERS: Beatrice Vincenzini, Mark Magowan, and Francesco Venturi

EDITOR: Jacqueline Decter
PRODUCTION DIRECTOR: Jim Spivey
DESIGNER: Rita Sowins / Sowins Design
WRITERS: Mitchell Owens and Hadley Keller

Library of Congress Cataloging-in-Publication Data available upon request

Distributed in North America by:
Abrams Books
www.abramsbooks.com

Distributed in the rest of the world by:
Thames & Hudson Ltd.
6–24 Britannia Street
London WC1X 9JD
United Kingdom
www.thamesandhudson.com

EU Authorized Representative:
Interart S.A.R.L.
19 Rue Charles Auray
93500 Pantin, Paris
France
productsafety@vendomepress.com
www.interart.fr

Printed and bound in China by RR Donnelley (Guangdong) Printing Solutions

First printing

PHOTO CREDITS

© John Merkl: 2–3, 6–7, 16–49

© Douglas Friedman: 4–5, 8, 12, 15, 50–109, 126–49, 162–79, 210–31, 260–78

© Trevor Tondro: 10, 110–25, 150–61, 198–209, 232–59

© Oscar Flink: 139

© Björn Wallander: 180–97

PAGES 2–3: Vaulted ceilings and textural wood floors—offset by bold art—embody the contemporary rustic aesthetic that the client envisioned for this house in Beverly Hills, which we designed with architect Richard Landry.

PAGES 4–5: In my own Palm Springs home, what was once a maze of dark, low-ceilinged rooms is now an airy living space imbued with sculptural forms and art that John and I passionately collect.

PAGES 6–7: In the heart of California wine country, I worked with architect Kirby Lee, formerly of Howard Backen's architectural firm, to create a large family estate that offered an incomparable indoor-outdoor living experience and set the stage for the clients' eclectic collection of vintage and contemporary European furniture.

PAGE 8: Our creative solution for warming up a minimalist home: commission an artist to create a brutalist-inspired wall collage of wood pieces as the backdrop to a dramatic staircase.

PAGE 10: A monumental Charles Arnoldi painting is a colorful counterpoint to the desert landscape outside this midcentury home in the storied Thunderbird Country Club in Rancho Mirage, near Palm Springs.

PAGE 12: A theatrical assemblage of art and antiques greets visitors at this desert estate, which we designed near the turn of the twenty-first century and continue to support with our design services.

PAGE 15: Turning every view inside a home into an artful moment is one of the hallmarks of my work.

PAGE 278: Sheldon Harte (left) and John Combs, outside their Palm Springs home.